The Journey of A Teenage Mother

16 Stories of Triumph Against the Odds

LaShunda Leslie-Smith, LMSW

with contributing authors

ISBN-13: 978-0615811499 (LaShunda Leslie-Smith, LMSW)
ISBN-10: 0615811493

DISCLAIMER: This book details each author's personal experiences with and opinions about teenage pregnancy. The primary author and publisher do not certify each author's story as factual, but rather it is each author's personal account of their life story. The authors are not licensed as educational consultants, teachers, psychologists, or psychiatrists.

Edited by Rebecca Chalone
Cover designed by A'Sista Media Group, LLC

DEDICATION

To my son Branden who kept me close to Jesus and who from the beginning inspired me to shine. My success is due to your existence.

CONTENTS

Never be afraid to trust an unknown future to a known God
Corrie ten Boom

ACKNOWLEDGMENTS

To God, the creator of the Universe and the head of my life…thank you! This project is a direct result of God's leading and His divine inspiration. To my husband, Moses Smith, who has shown unconditional love through every storm and who has brought great joy into my life. To my children, Branden and Myanna, I am proud to be your momma. You two are my greatest accomplishments! To my mother, Carolyn, I love you more than you will ever know. To my dad, Daniel Leslie, thank you for showing a little girl true love and for setting the bar high for the man who came into my life. To Necole and EJ, I have always tried to be the best example possible to the two of you, I hope you feel I was able to accomplish that goal. To my besties, Martha, Olivia, and Janelle, thank you for laugher, late night prayer sessions, and sharing tears of joy and sadness with me. To my prayer partners, Julie, Michelle, Maria, and Danielle thank you for lifting me up…always. To my sister-girl, assistant, makeup artist, and travel buddy, Yolanda! I love you to life! A special thank you to Cindy Lumpkin as well as Olivia West for assisting me through this process. I am forever grateful to God for bringing Debbie, Maisha, Tiffiney, Elizabeth, LaToya, Tanishia, Charlyn, Sarah-Elizabeth, Stephanie, Nikki, Rosa, Shenita, and Shiera into my life. This project would be nothing without you ladies. I also want to thank Branden and Rafael for being brave young soldiers and sharing your stories as well. Thank you!

A Woman Who Once Was A Girl

You have made her into a woman,
A woman, a woman, who once was a girl.
One who struggled to find herself.
One, who knew too much, saw too much, heard too much,
Struggled too much.
Thought life would be easier if she could just get out.
Took a route that changed her life.
Some thought for the worse,
But she could handle strife.
Young girl with a baby, what will she do, how can she make it?
Even when she wasn't feeling good, she tried to fake it.
Life never got easier, it got harder and harder.
But with the help of the Lord she became
A woman, a woman, a woman
Who once was a girl.
A young girl with grown up responsibilities,
Who despite all odds, acknowledged her capabilities, and persevered.
She is now a woman, a woman, a woman,
Who once was a girl.
Where is the father? Long gone from here.
Her testimony is graciously owed to The God in her life.
He wiped her tears when they fell at night.
Baby boy gave her new hope,
He cheered her on at her high school graduation.
Having him became her true inspiration,
To move through the stages of life,
That helped her to become
A woman, a woman, a woman
Who once was a girl.

-LaShunda Leslie-Smith © 2005

FOREWORD

DR. MELANIE WATKINS
Physician, Author, and Speaker

LaShunda Leslie-Smith, LMSW, along with 16 contributing authors, have written a book to help readers gain an inside view as to what life is like as a teenage mother. Through the paragraphs and the poetry, LaShunda takes the reader back to her childhood and lays the foundation for how she found herself pregnant at just 14 years old. Fast forward to the present day and she is a successful author, speaker and non-profit executive who has a loving relationship with her husband and children and now is in a position to "pay it forward" and to help other young mothers see the opportunities that are available to them. The book provides important insights and examples of women who have dealt with teen pregnancy and emerged stronger and more capable as a result of the personal growth they experienced.

In sharp contrast to *16 and Pregnant*, there is no glamour or television created drama. There are stories of young women facing domestic violence, living on public assistance, and dealing with appropriate boundaries. These are real stories, testimonies to how spiritual faith and community can make all the difference for a young mother.

As a former teen mother and author of Taking My Medicine: My Journey from Teenage Mother to Physician, I had to work through the significant logistical, emotional, and financial challenges that raising a child as an adolescent brings. Despite significant challenges, I, like LaShunda, relied on my personal relationship with my higher power, mentorship, and community support to overcome obstacles to pursue my dream of going to Stanford University Medical School and to become a physician.

As a psychiatrist reviewing this book, I can see how several factors early on in the lives of some of these young women may have led them down the path of getting involved in difficult relationships. Teen pregnancy can happen to young women from any socioeconomic or cultural background. The reader can appreciate how each woman developed the confidence that comes only after one triumphs over hurdles and disappointments. The reader can also appreciate the resilience these young women develop as they learn who they are and learn what it takes to move them forward in life, whether that be the decision to leave an abusive relationship, pursue their education, assert themselves, and/or advocate for their child(ren).

The common theme for many of these young women is faith, which was instrumental in my own success. The reader will gain valuable insight as to what led these young women to make the decisions they made and how they were able to get back on track, when it was very easy to get derailed. Not only will this book bring hope to young women currently expecting or parenting, but also for those who mentor them and guide them, professionally and personally. Uniquely, the reader is given the perspective of three grown children of former teen mothers. Statistically, women who pursue their education have children who are less likely to become young parents themselves.

This book is timely because teenage pregnancy still presents challenges that we all have to deal with as a society. How do we connect with young women to help them make decisions that are in their own best interest and will help their children lead the best lives they can? How do we assist them with pursuing their education? How do we help reduce stigma? How do we break the cycle of young women having not one, but two or three children in their late teens? Timeless questions with which those working with teenage mothers are all too familiar. After reading this book, the reader will gain an inside view as to what these women really face on a day to day basis as young women trying to grow and develop while also raising a child.

I was touched to have an opportunity to read this book, one in which young women allow themselves to be vulnerable so that their stories can be heard and understood by others. Many will identify with the struggles these women face as they learn their own identity and roles in this world. I applaud Mrs. Leslie Smith for her efforts in discussing this important and timely topic, which not only affects young women, but our society as a whole.

As Sarah-Elizabeth, one of the authors, reminds us, yes, all things are possible through Him. With faith, God will place the people you need, the resources you need, and the experiences you need to reach what may seem to be impossible goals. This book is an excellent example of the greatness that can come when one implements that faith!

Psychiatrist, Author, and Speaker
www.takingmymedicine.com
www.facebook.com/mwatkinsmd
www.drmelaniewatkins.com

ONE

JOURNEY OF A TEENAGE MOTHER
LaShunda Leslie-Smith

There I was, crying as hard as anyone could. I am so grateful to God for bringing me out. How would I have made it if I did not put my trust in the Lord? I remember screaming to myself, *I hate her! I do not want to live here anymore. I am going to run away. Just wait. No one wants me here anyway.*

I packed my things when no one was home. The next morning, I got up for school in a good mood. *I'm going to break out of jail today,* I mused to myself.

My mother got up and made coffee like she normally did.

My stepfather was away at work. He was a truck driver and he stayed gone for two, sometimes three weeks at a time. Some of those weeks were probably spent with other women. I didn't care. The longer he stayed away, the better. He and my mom had been together since I was about two or three; I couldn't recall exactly. But what I do remember was that he had always been in my life. My biological father, on the other hand, was a different story. I didn't ever remember him and my mother being together.

He, my *real* dad, lived in California all my life. I got to see him some summers. I can only remember one occasion as a child when I saw him in New York. His father had died and he had flown to New York to attend the funeral.

As soon as my mother jumped into the shower, I snuck outside and hid the bag of clothes I'd packed. I was 12 or 13 years old and in the 7th grade. I went back into the house and finished getting ready for school.

"I'm leaving mom," I said.

"Ok. Have a good day," she replied walking me to the door.

She was in a good mood. Why? I wasn't sure. I almost felt bad for leaving. She wasn't evil *all* the time. There were times when she could be really nice

"No, no, not this time! You are leaving." I yelled to myself. "She is not going to Dr. Jekyll and Mrs. Hyde me today!"

Her personality changes, the violence and all of the fighting—I just couldn't take it anymore. She and her crazy husband deserved each other! But I did hate leaving my younger siblings behind, especially my little sister—we're six years apart. She was so young and she hated to hear them fighting. My little brother and I were not that close, nonetheless, I was still very concerned for both of their welfare.

In my house, because I was the oldest, I had a lot of responsibility. My siblings were more like my children at times. I was expected to discipline them when my parents weren't home. I had to feed them, bathe them, and look after them. My mother made it very clear: if something went wrong, I would get the blame. When my parents were home, things were different. All that power I had when they weren't around? Gone. I was not allowed to discipline them, and she reminded me of that all of the time.

"These are *my* kids," she would say. It wasn't that my mother did not take responsibility for all of us; but being a child myself, I felt she placed too much responsibility on me, especially when it came to caring for my younger siblings. One day I was momma, the next, I was sister. I often felt very confused about my role in our family.

After saying goodbye, I started walking down the street as if I were on my way to catch the bus to school. When I saw that my mother closed the door, I turned around, ran back to the house as fast as I could, grabbed the bag of clothes I had hidden outside, and then ran for the school bus. This was the first time I had ever run away. I didn't look back.

It was the last day of the school year. I only went to school that day to take my final exams. I had no clue where I was going to go or whom I was going to stay with. I had no money for food nor did I have money to catch the bus. Still, I was not afraid. I felt free. I was happy to be out of my parent's home. Nothing else mattered at that point. Being on my own, even though that was short lived, gave me great peace of mind—more than I ever experienced.

My life on the run ended prematurely after I called an aunt. She shared that my mother was grief stricken. She thought that I had been kidnapped, raped, or possibly killed. Even though she couldn't protect herself from abuse, my mother was very protective of us. The thought of her suffering, of her grieving, was enough to convince me to go back home. I'd been gone from home for less than 12 hours. I never even expected her to miss me.

I lived in a home plagued by domestic violence. My parents would fight all the time and I'm not just talking about loud arguments. My stepfather had a nasty temper. In the streets, at home, it didn't matter. His temper was exacerbated when he drank or did drugs, or sometimes did both. Simple things set him off. If my mother did not have dinner ready on time, there was a great possibility that a fist fight would be in store before the night was over.

Domestic violence is an ugly thing. Most parents don't realize the impact it has on the children who witness it. My earliest memory of my stepfather beating my mother was when I was about 5 years old. I was awakened by my stepfather who was inquiring of my mother's whereabouts that day. I could hardly understand what he was asking, having been shaken out of my sleep. I tried explaining that we were at the shop all day, my grandmother's beauty salon. My grandmother owned two beauty salons in the city and we spent a lot of time in them. My grandmother was often my saving grace. My stepfather did not believe me. He repeatedly asked me where we had been that day. I tried to explain. He was not happy with my response.

Even at the age of five, I somehow understood that his own guilt caused him to behave this way. Still not happy with my response, he proceeded to interrogate my mother about where she had been. She replied over and over that she had been with her mother all day at the shop. He was consumed with anger. I don't think it even mattered what she said at that point. He was ready to explode. He walked away for a while. It was clear that he had been drinking. When he drank, he was not a nice person to be around. I never understood why my mother never said enough is enough!

As an adult, I realize now that her own insecurities caused her to put up with the abuse. The fact that he made a really good living driving trucks and was a good provider to our home, made the decision of leaving him even more difficult. At the time, I thought that she didn't want to give up her fairy tale life of having a husband, a house, two cars, three kids, and a dog (even though the dog only lasted a little while). I thought she cared more about the American dream than she did about her own welfare or that of her children.

I think my mother found comfort in the fact that my stepfather never abused us. In fact, he was good to us and showed us that he loved us. I loved him too and still do. But when I was a child, I didn't like him for what he did to my mother. At times, I hated him. Truth is, I never really blamed him as much as I did my mother…she was the one who stayed.

That night my stepfather was just looking for something to argue about. He got upset about dinner not being done and when my mother got up to prepare dinner, he jumped in her face. It was an intense moment and there was nothing I could do to protect my mother. I can only imagine what might have been going through her mind at the time.

She proceeded to the kitchen, and he followed her. From the living room, I could hear him slap her.

She started screaming, "What did I do?"

As if there were ever a good reason for a man to slap a woman. He hit her again and again. She ran out of the kitchen and attempted to flee up the stairs to the second floor. He caught her and punched her in her thighs repeatedly.

He beat her over and over as I watched, helplessly crying, "Please stop, don't hurt my mommy."

As I think back on this incident, I realize now my mother's concern at the time was always for her safety. I don't ever remember her trying to protect me or my siblings or her being concerned that we were in the middle of this mess. Memories like this one, and many others, still burn in my mind today. I often weep for my mother, and the woman she was before the abuse.

A Letter to My Mother

A letter to my mother, no not a love letter,
Wishing it were, but there is nothing better
Than getting off my chest those things held for years,
As I reminisce, my eyes swell with tears.
A letter to my mother, you were that rock for years,
But your spirit was weakened by him, as he banged upside your head;
You bled,
Right before my eyes.
A letter to my mother, no surprise, that you returned once again,
Even as a little girl I wondered when will this end?
My minded flooded with thoughts of your demise,
Who will take care of us, who will supply,
All the needs that you fulfilled,
The days of our lives, shortened by your choices,
Limited by those voices
That whispered I will be the same,
The only hope I had was to call upon His name,
Jesus!

Heal this frightened little girl,
Whose world has been turned upside down,
Choices made by others threatening to put me in the ground.
This is a letter to my mother, no, not a love letter,
But something much better.
It is a letter of forgiveness, of hope and of joy,
Something those hidden skeletons in our closets threatened to destroy.
This is a letter to my mother, and in spite of those hard times,
I haven't forgotten those things you taught me.
Your lessons, your love, your guidance, and how far it's brought me.
You are a beautiful woman, your skin kissed by the sun,
I looked up to you and the day has come,
I, now a mother, with a daughter just like me.
I learned from your mistakes and never will there be,
A time when she will wonder about the future of her mother.
This is a letter to my mother, your sins uncovered,
Forgiven and forgotten to be remembered no more.
Our future is bright and hope has been restored.
This is a letter to my mother.

-LaShunda Leslie-Smith © 2012

I never thought I could please my mother and I often felt out of place in my immediate family, being the only child with a different father. My father lived so far away. Although he was a good man, there was a period of time when we had no communication.

My parent's home caught on fire when I was in second or third grade. My mother claimed that my father's phone number was burned in the house fire and she could no longer reach him. I don't know if attempts were made by my father to reach me during that period of time. I can only hope that he searched high and low for me—his little girl, his only child. I was in the sixth grade when I was united with my paternal family. Two of my paternal aunts and my paternal grandmother flew to Rochester to search for me. I don't know how they found me, but I remember that day like it was yesterday. I was in the kitchen washing dishes when I heard the doorbell ring. I went to the door and saw my aunt Darlene standing at the steps. I paused for a moment, thinking perhaps I was dreaming.

She said through the screen door, "Do you remember me?"

I smiled, and opened the screen door and said, "Yes!"

I can remember that as being one of the best summers of my life. Later that summer, I flew to California to be reunited with my dad. It was an awesome feeling and we have never been out of contact since. Being apart from my father for such a long period of time left a hole in my heart, one that could not be fulfilled by the family that I lived with. Certainly, my mother loved me, but she wasn't excited about sharing me with my father. As we were on the way to the airport, she suddenly turned to me and said with clenched teeth, "You better not go to California and tell them you want to live there. I raised you all these years and I will not let them take you away from me."

I am sure my mother's attempt to scare me was motivated by her own fear of losing me. She never had the words to express her love to a child in a gentle and appropriate way. Perhaps she never got what she needed as a child and therefore had little to offer us. Perhaps that was the reason she settled for the kind of love offered to her by my stepfather, or the other men to come, who would not appreciate her value, her beauty, and her undeniable intelligence.

"You better come back," she told me. I was terrified of my mother and I intended to do what she said!

I often wonder what my life would be like today had I remained in California for the rest of my upbringing. I certainly would not have met Bradley. Still, the wounds in my heart and soul had already begun to ooze. California or not, I probably would have met someone just like Bradley. Someone who said the right things, at the right time, to a broken little girl.

I really wish my mother had been emotionally available to support me through challenging times as I grew into a young woman. There were no talks about boys, sex, dating, or the like. I was left to explore on my own. My counselors were other sexually confused seventh and eighth graders. I attended an inner-city middle school where just about everyone had given up their virginity by the seventh grade, or at least that was the lie they all told. I was criticized by friends, because at the ripe old age of 13, I was still a virgin. No one taught me the importance of this gift, or the importance of why it was specifically meant for my husband. Without hesitation, and in an attempt to be deemed cool, I gave my precious gift to someone whose name I don't even remember. I had seen many things in my short life, but I was not prepared for what was yet to come.

At age 13, I met Bradley, a young man who used to hang out next door to a relative's home. He was the bad-boy type. He smoked, drank, was a high school dropout, and was pretty much living on his own because his mother was a crack addict. He was by all definitions, a lost boy, and just perfect for a lost girl.

I really liked Bradley. He was charming, fun to be around, and he said nice things to me. Looking back, I can't blame myself for choosing someone like Bradley or anyone else who gave me attention. I have learned from working with hundreds of teenage girls that we are all in search of something. For some its acceptance, for some its love, and for some it's a sense of identity. I think I was looking for all three.

Bradley and I began to date exclusively and within two months of dating him, I was pregnant with his child. I was 14 years old and in the eighth grade. I gave birth four days before my 15th birthday. Prior to getting pregnant, I moved out of my parent's home and in with my grandmother. I could no longer deal with the issues that plagued me at home. Just before I gave birth to Branden, my mother asked me to move back in, and so I did. Surprisingly, our relationship had improved by me living outside of her home. Not surprisingly, it began to deteriorate when I moved back. My mother's lack of control over her own life, specifically her marriage, often meant she overcompensated by trying to control us kids. By the time my son was 9 months old, I moved out again. This time I moved in with an aunt and Bradley moved in with me.

We played house until I moved out on my own. When I was 16, I applied for temporary assistance through the Department of Social Services and was able to move into my own apartment. Bradley and I were beginning to grow apart. I was trying to finish school and he saw no interest in that. When I would share my dreams about owning my own home, his responses were always negative. I stayed, despite the fact that we were growing apart, because we had a son to raise. I was determined to raise my son with Bradley and not by myself. It wasn't long before I realized Bradley wasn't ready to change. He wasn't ready to be the man, or the father, my son and I needed. He had no plans of returning to school, he had no job, and the jobs he had had in the past, he'd always quit. He would street hustle to help buy diapers and clothes for our son, but I didn't want any part of that lifestyle. One of the best decisions I made was not giving Bradley a key to my apartment and not allowing him to move in, although he would stay the night from time to time. It was the separation and independence I needed to eventually end that relationship.

As I grew in my independence, Bradley became controlling. One day I discovered money missing from my coat pocket and I asked him about it. He was very defensive, but eventually stated that he had taken it and he didn't see anything wrong in having done so. I was furious. I explained that that money was for the house, for diapers, and even for food. He showed no remorse. He just looked past me, continuing to watch TV as if I were invisible. At that moment I knew, this was not the plan God had for me. I asked him to leave, this time for good. Unfortunately, he borrowed my house key earlier that day. I asked him to return it and he refused. I went to my room and threatened to call the police if he didn't leave. He followed me back to the room, and, using profane language, threatened to punch me in the face if I called the police. I was scared, again. I told him that I wasn't going to call the police, that instead I was calling my mother. I didn't know where that side of Bradley had come from. He was normally a gentle person. I called my mother while she was at work. I shared with her what was going on as tears streaked my face. My voice shook. She could identify with this kind of pain. She immediately left work and came to my rescue. Bradley left before she arrived.

She told me to pack some clothes because she didn't want me staying in the apartment alone that night. I did what she asked. After all, she had done this a hundred times before. As my son and I drove off in my mother's car, fleeing the place that once represented peace and safety, I reminisced about the many times my siblings and I had fled our home with my mother. In and out of battered women's shelters we'd gone. I knew that I did not want that for my child.

The next day I went to a hardware store and purchased supplies to change my locks. I called Bradley and told him that he could no longer stay the night, and, in fact, he was no longer welcomed in my home. I made it clear that I was not scared of him and that I would not put up with his abuse. That day, I made a decision. I would not allow history to repeat itself. I didn't understand how much dead weight Bradley was in my life until I left him for good. I determined that if I were ever going to tell my son to go to school and do well, I too would have to go to school and do well. And so I did! It was not easy, but somehow I found the strength to move past the difficult days, which made the good days easy to celebrate.

I met my best friend Martha Williams the same year I left Bradley. She was very quiet and a bit strange. She talked about church all the time and encouraged me to attend with her.

I would always say to her, "I'll burn up if I walked through church doors!" She was forgiving, encouraging, and she never judged my life style. What she did, which meant so much to me, was to set an example of what it meant to be a Christian rather than telling me. Her entire life style was a testimony of who God was and is.

The summer between tenth and eleventh grade, Martha and I were determined to find jobs. She learned that Seabreeze Amusement Park was hiring and she and I went to apply. We both got jobs and began working right away. It was the worst job I'd had to date! But it turned out to be one of the best things that ever happened to me. It was there that I met another really good friend, Olivia Bradley. Olivia and I connected immediately; she had a personality larger than life. That summer I also met a guy named Moses. Moses was a nice guy, but didn't immediately strike me as my type. However, we did have this unbelievable connection. We grew close as friends and spent a lot of time together during our breaks at work and on the phone in the evenings. Eventually, I asked Moses to meet Branden and it was love at first sight. I had no clue that I would spend the rest of my life with this man.

Moses supported me through every major milestone in my life, even the little ones. He took on Branden as his own son. I would laugh when strangers in the park would say to him, "Your son looks just like you." They couldn't tell that Branden was not his biological child and neither could I.

Life was starting to feel balanced. My son was healthy and thriving. I was in a healthy committed relationship with a man who respected women and honored his responsibilities (thank God for my wonderful mother-in-law). I was maintaining my independence, although it was still a struggle at times. I was employed and able to support myself and my son with little assistance from the government. I was proud. Those feelings of shame and guilt for being *the girl who got pregnant in the eighth grade* weren't so prevalent anymore. Still, there was a missing piece.

When I was 17 years old, I felt a tugging at my heart. The life that I had made for myself was not a bad one, but it wasn't always pleasing to the Lord either. I had shut God out of my life. But the Word says in John 12:32, "And I, if I am lifted up from the earth, I will draw all men to Myself." I thank God for the praying mothers and grandmothers of the world who stand in the gap for the lost boys and lost girls, who sometimes become lost men and lost women. I was indeed a lost woman. That year someone invited me to the Church of Love Faith Center on Brooks Ave, in Rochester, New York. Reluctantly, I attended. I don't remember that person ever attending a single service after that, but I never stopped going. Once again, I was totally unprepared for what was to come after surrendering my life to the Lord.

It was because of my relationship with Jesus Christ that the chains of poverty, fornication, and out of wedlock pregnancy were broken. Speaking prophetically, chains and generational curses will not repeat themselves in the lives of my children. Moses eventually gave his life to the Lord as well. Moses and I married shortly after. I was 19 at the time and he was 24. We recently celebrated 15 years of marriage. He continues to fill the role of father for Branden and together we have a daughter who is now 12 years old. She adores her daddy. Our life, though not perfect, is a true testament of Gods faithfulness to those who serve Him.

Though my relationship with my mother is still not where I would like it to be, she respects me as an adult woman and I, though I don't always agree with them, respect the life choices she makes. More than anything, I love her. A little piece of me still seeks her undivided love, attention and approval - things I may never get. I am fortunate to have always had a relationship with my dad, despite the long distance. He is a wonderful, God fearing man. Although we still live miles apart, he has never missed a graduation or a major milestone for me or for my children. We are closer now that I am an adult than we could have ever been when I was younger. There is nothing that could separate him and me and I am extremely proud to call him my father. Surprisingly, I also have a good relationship with my stepfather. Despite the pain he caused my mother, he was still a big part of my life growing up. We don't see each other often, but my kids know him as Grampy and my husband I and stop by to see him and his wife from time to time. When I gave my life to the Lord, God took the pain and hurt that I had endured at the hands of other people and filled that void with love. I am proud to say that I have forgiven everyone who I feel wronged me in the past. I have moved on. I have been set free!

Here I am who once was pregnant in the eighth grade, a teen mother, a welfare recipient, a child of a battered mother, a single parent, one who struggled academically and with low self-esteem and with low self-image, and one who shed many tears over countless hurts. Yet I am proud to say that I don't look like what I've been through. I have turned my pain into purpose and my mess into my ministry. I now hold a bachelor's degree, a master's degree, and I have PhD courses under my belt. I am a wife to a wonderful man and a mother of two beautiful children. I am proud to call them my own. I am an executive, an entrepreneur, a public speaker, and an author. I am an agent of change!

I don't boast to say, "Look at me!" I am simply who I was made to be and that is a great feeling! I am no longer that broken, hurt, and confused little girl. I am a confident God-fearing woman who can conquer anything set before me. I am, simply because He is!

It is my hope that my story and the stories of the women and young men in this book would bless you beyond measure.

Author's Corner

Biography: LaShunda Leslie-Smith earned a Bachelor of Arts in psychology with a minor in child and family services from St. John Fisher College, a Masters in Social Work from the Greater Rochester Collaborative Master of Social Work Program, and a certificate in non-profit leadership from Roberts Wesleyan College. LaShunda developed her passion for youth and the human service field through her roles as a child protective investigator for Monroe County Department of Human Services and a therapeutic foster care social worker for Hillside Family of Agencies. LaShunda's nonprofit management and fundraising skills were further developed in her role as Executive Director of Successful Pathways, an organization that she founded. Her responsibilities include overall agency management, human resources, program development, grant compliance, marketing and fundraising. In February of 2007, LaShunda was named one of Rochester, New York's Emerging African American Leaders, by the *Democrat and Chronicle*. She has been featured in *Rochester Insider* magazine, and was named the Woman in the Spotlight by the Women's Council of Rochester, NY. In 2008, the *Rochester Insider* magazine named Ms. Leslie-Smith, Most Likely to Succeed. In 2009 she was named a Woman to Watch by *HerRochester*. The City of Rochester, awarded LaShunda the 2011 Pioneer Award for the youth work that she does in Rochester. Committed to her community, LaShunda serves on several boards and committees. She also serves in multiple ministries at the Church of Love Faith Center. LaShunda is a motivational speaker, author, and consultant. LaShunda is blessed to share her life's journey with her husband Moses Smith and their two children, Branden and Myanna.

The young do not know enough to be prudent, and therefore they attempt the impossible - and achieve it, generation after generation.
Pearl S. Buck

TWO

MORE THAN A STATISTIC
Stephanie Motley

"Now that you are pregnant I just want you to promise me one thing, to be more than a statistic."

These were the words my aunt said to me when I informed her that I was pregnant. How did I get to that point, you ask? Well, let me tell you about my journey of becoming a teenage mother.

One night, I was on a four way call with my boyfriend at the time, my best friend, and her boyfriend. We were having one of our normal funny conversations, until the subject of sex came up. The guys asked my best friend if she planned to wait until marriage before having sex.

My best friend replied, "I would like to, but what if my husband does not have what it takes to satisfy me?" We all laughed and told her she was crazy even though we knew she was very serious. Then it was my turn to answer the question.

"I would love to wait until marriage," I said. "But let's be real for a moment, many people do not reach that goal. But I do want to wait until I am at least twenty-seven years old."

"Twenty-seven?" Everyone asked in disbelief.

"Yes, twenty-seven," I replied. "I want to wait until I graduate from college and have started my career, then if I were to get pregnant, I could afford it."

"Oh, okay, I understand now. At first I just wondered why you picked such a random number," said my best friend.

They picked on me for so long about my picking a random age to have sex. But twelve years before age twenty-seven, I lost my virginity. On Black Friday, in 2005, I gave my virginity to my boyfriend after a year and four months of dating. Did I do it because I was ready? No. Was I really sure what I was getting myself into? No. Why did I do it? Well, I had allowed him to touch me, kiss me, and pursue sexual contact with me up to the point of intercourse and for me to stop him from going all the way would have made him mad because he would have felt like I was a tease; or so I thought. I did not want him to think I was a tease or to get mad at me and get "it" from someone else. I convinced myself that it was okay to go ahead and have sex with him because I loved him and we had been together for over a year, so I knew he loved me too.

I took a deep breath and told him, "Okay, I'm ready."

That was the biggest lie I have ever told in my life. I closed my eyes, took a deep breath and rivers of tears flowed down my face until it was over.

The next day I had so many mixed feelings I cannot even begin to name them all. The feeling I felt the most was disappointment. I was disappointed in myself because I did the very thing I said I would not do. I gave up my virginity before I was ready and it was just to keep him from being mad. The next day I interrogated myself.

How could you have been so stupid? How could you have allowed this to happen? I demanded of myself *Do I still have value?* I asked. *Will anyone be able to tell? Is he going to want to do this all the time? Is this what our relationship is going to be based on now? Did he tell his friends? Where do we go from here? Is God mad at me? Ugh! What did I do?*

Finally, I stopped asking myself questions and prepared for play practice at my church. Our Christmas play was soon to come and there was no way I could remember all my lines, especially thinking about the fact that I had just had sex for the first time.

When I got to play practice, the first person I saw was my best friend. I battled in my head whether or not I should tell her. I wondered if I told her, would it make her do it too? I didn't want that, but I needed someone to talk to about what had just happened. Once practice was over, I pulled her to the side and told her what had happened.

The first thing that came out of her mouth was, "I thought you were going to wait until you were twenty-seven?"

I could not do anything but laugh. "So much for that," I replied.

She asked me the common questions like what was it like, and how did it feel, but ironically, I couldn't tell her because I didn't know. My mind had been so focused on how wrong I was that I could not have enjoyed it.

"Oh, naw honey, it must not have been good then," my best friend said with this *you can't be serious* look on her face.

Basketball season was about to start and I was so glad. This would occupy my time and make me unavailable to have sex on a regular basis. This was my last season on the Junior Varsity team, second year as captain, and it was my year to shine. I planned to do just that. Basketball was my passion at the time.

As captain of the team, I tried to be a great leader for my fellow teammates. I did not give any sign of being sexually active. I presented myself as a mature, hardworking student athlete. We had a good season. I finished my last season as a Junior Varsity player with a bang. The last game of the season, I hit a half-court shot at the buzzer, created some nice plays, and hit the majority of the shots I put up. I just knew that a varsity jersey had my name on it for next season. Shockingly, I did not have to wait until the next season. I was moved up to varsity for the play-offs. Even though I didn't get any playing time, I was grateful to be able to dress up and warm up with the varsity team. We were the Dogwood District Champions that year and made it to the regional play-offs. Junior varsity and varsity girls were not just teammates, we were family. We had a bond that was not going to be broken until graduation, or so we thought.

November 2006 rolled around and it was try out time again. I spent the entire summer preparing myself for this moment by improving my left hand skills, playing summer league for a more intense experience, exercising, and staying in shape. I felt like I had it in the bag. As tryouts began, I started to feel uncomfortable. Every time the varsity coach demonstrated a drill I would pay close attention. I even watched the people in front of me do it repeatedly to make sure I understood correctly. Yet, it seemed that when it became my turn, I could never do it to his satisfaction. He would yell at me more than the others. It just seemed like I was being singled out. Despite how I was feeling, I still persevered and continued doing my best each day at try-outs. The time came to reveal the names for the team. If you made the team, your name would be on the list hanging on the wall. If you did not make it, your name would not be on the list. You had to get your stuff and leave. Once the list was posted, all the girls took off to see if their names were listed. I, on the other hand, took my time because I had noticed a little debate between the varsity coach, his assistant, (which was his son), and my junior varsity coach which had left my coach sitting alone with tears in his eyes. Once I stood directly in front of the list, I searched for my name. It wasn't there. In that moment, my dreams died; my journey to varsity level was gone. My chance to play for the University of North Carolina Chapel Hill was over and I did not know how to handle that. Before I allowed my emotions to get the best of me I grabbed my stuff and ran to my car. *How could this be? How could I not be on the team? After three years of loyalty to junior varsity, two years as captain, MVP the previous season, and promoted to varsity for the playoffs last season and I didn't make it?* Only thirteen girls tried out and they had fifteen jerseys. There was plenty of room to keep me. I was the only one they had cut for varsity. How did they not have room for me? The pain I felt that day was like nothing I had ever felt before. My dream was over.

Now that I did not play basketball anymore, I had a void that I needed to fill. I did not feel complete anymore. I felt like something was missing. I turned to spending more time with my boyfriend which also led to having more sex. I was having sex up to four times a week. It was my new way of coping with problems. Other people turned to drugs and alcohol, but for me, sex was all I thought I needed .

In February of 2007, I was helping one of my friends throw her father a surprise birthday party. We both noticed that my weight had picked up and I would get tired and have to sit down often.

She asked, "Are you sure you are not pregnant?"

I answered, "Girl, no, I just need to lose some weight. The test read negative back in January."

People started to arrive at the party. The more children at the party, the more irritated I became. I did not understand why I felt that way because I had always loved kids. So I told my friend that something was not right because my stomach felt weird every time I got close to a child. She told me we needed to go get a test. I refused. She asked me when was the last time I had had a menstrual cycle. I informed her that I had not had one since November. She looked at me like she could have slapped me. She called her older cousin in the back room with us and told her what was going on.

She asked me about possible symptoms and after my answer was yes to all of them she said, "Yes, honey, you are pregnant."

I believed her because she had two children of her own, but I still needed a test to confirm it. We left the party to go get the test and came back so I could take it. After waiting two minutes, which seemed like two hours, we looked at the test. Due to deep denial, I still read the test as negative. My two witnesses, however, read it correctly. My heart dropped to the floor. I just knew my life was over. I picked up the phone to tell my boyfriend that I was pregnant.

In shock he told me, "You can't keep it."

Then, after taking a deep breath, he told me, "Let me call you back, I have to gather my thoughts." After about fifteen minutes, he called back and asked me if I was okay and told me not to worry and that everything was going to be okay. My ears heard what he said but my heart was still heavy. I felt like an even bigger failure especially since not making the varsity team. I knew the disappointment would only grow once I told my parents, my sister, and the rest of my family. I would have to face the youth choir at my church and tell them that I, their president, was expecting and see more disappointment. My life was shattering before my eyes and I did not know how to stop it. I became so depressed that I would cry myself to sleep. Even though my family said they were going to be by my side, I still felt that this baby was going to change my life for the worse. Instead, it was the total opposite.

On August 23, 2007, I gave birth to the most beautiful creation I had ever seen. Semiyah Michelle Royal graced this world at 5lbs 7oz and 23½ inches long. In that moment, all the depression, the disappointments, the negative comments, and the humility went away. Love came over me and it was a love that I had never received or given before. When she arrived she brought a joy that I had never had, a determination that basketball had never given, and a motivation that no friend, family member, or boyfriend had ever brought into my life.

Being a mom took a while to get used to. There were plenty of times that I wanted to go out but I could not. I needed to be at home with my daughter. Having a job was now mandatory and not an option. Balancing school, a job, and motherhood took a lot out of me each and every day but I was determined to do it. In 2009, I lost my job. I was devastated. I had a child to take care of. Yes, I still lived at home with my mother; however, it was my obligation to take care of Semiyah, not anyone else's. I was without a job for an entire year and it was a very low and depressing year for me. All I wanted to do was provide for my daughter but doing it without a job was very difficult. There were plenty of times that I needed to buy pampers or milk and had to find ways to do it without asking my parents. Due to a lack of full coverage insurance and no Medicaid coverage, my parents had to pay all my medical bills out of pocket. Therefore, I did things such as sell the music system out of my car, my stereo, and my jewelry to be able to purchase the necessities for my daughter without asking my parents. I also had great friends and family who would pitch in at times and help me. I was truly blessed to have a great support system. Semiyah's father would pitch in at times. However, the majority of the time his mother would do his part for him. She was there every step of the way just like my parents. As I think back now, I believe my daughter's father was the father he knew how to be at the time. We were very young and we were both trying to figure out the whole "parent thing." His father had never really played the father role in his life; instead, he played the friend role. Therefore, my daughter's father had to learn on his own what it meant to be a good father.

In 2010, a job finally came through for me. I was so happy. I didn't know what to do with myself. But, what seemed to be a breakthrough was the very thing that almost caused me to have a breakdown. The job I accepted was as an administrative assistant at a mental health company. I loved the job, after I became comfortable with it, but the treatment I received from my direct supervisor was not acceptable. I did not quit. I did not give up. I went back to what my mother instilled in me: prayer. I prayed and asked God to take me off my journey and place me on the journey He had for me. Physically, I was alive and well, but spiritually, I was dead. I needed to know my purpose. I wanted God to show me what He saw in me. After much prayer and fasting, God answered. I received another job, one that allowed me to work without being watched over. I am currently the HR manager and I treat all my employees with dignity and respect. Not only did God favor me with a managerial position without having a degree, He showed me my purpose in life of starting a non-profit organization by giving me a dream of helping single teen mothers who are facing the same struggles I faced. After writing out the vision of the non-profit organization, it was time to pick a title. Immediately my aunt's voice spoke to me so clearly and I heard her say, "...more than a statistic." Tears began to stream down my face. I was overwhelmed at the full circle that had occurred in my life.

Here it is a year later from starting a non-profit organization and I am part of this amazing opportunity of writing this book. I'm sharing my story with more girls than just the ones that reside within my city and surrounding areas. I found my purpose in life and God's journey for me is still being written.

Author's Corner

Biography: Stephanie was born on January 9, 1990 to Karen and Henry Motley, Jr.. She was baptized and became a member of Greater Triumph Missionary Baptist Church at the age of 4 under the leadership of the late Pastor H. G. McGhee, Sr.. From the age of 4, Stephanie started serving in the church by joining the youth choir. As she grew, her serving grew as well. She became a member of the hospitality committee, and eventually became a vacation Bible school teacher, youth Bible study teacher, president and director over the youth choir, and praise and worship leader. Stephanie is currently a member of the Smith Chapel Baptist Church where Rev. Jermaine Parker serves as Pastor. At Smith Chapel Baptist Church she serves as a member on the praise and worship team. Stephanie graduated from Chatham High School with an advanced diploma in 2008. She plans to further her education in physical therapy. Stephanie is currently employed at ATIBA Youth Interventions where she is the business manager and outreach coordinator. Stephanie is also the CEO/Founder of More Than A Statistic, LLC. More Than A Statistic is a nonprofit organization formed to be a support system to teens and single parents. Even though the nonprofit organization has only been established for a year, the name and mission of the organization has gained attention internationally. Stephanie was featured in the 2013 *Danville Edition Emerge Magazine* as the cover story. She was featured as a guest on *Blog Talk Radio* morning show *Me, God, and A Cup of Coffee* with host Susan Kee. Stephanie was also featured in an online magazine *Let's Chic Chat* with Ms. Jocelyn Saunders. Stephanie has a passion for inspiring, encouraging, and helping young ladies. She seeks to help the ladies of her generation realize their self worth and value and to not just settle for anything. Every opportunity she has to speak into a young ladies life she takes seriously. She thinks that this generation lacks the knowledge of who they really are and what their real purpose is in life. This generation of ladies is lost looking for love instead of being captured in the love of Jesus and allowing Him to reveal to them what real love is. She knows this, because at one point she was one of them.

Acknowledgments: Thanks to my mother and father, Karen and Henry Motley, Jr., for always supporting my dreams. Thank you to my sister and brother- in- law, Jessica and Courtney Hairston, for always supporting me and mentoring me. I want to give a huge thank you to my daughter, Semiyah Royal. You inspire me every day to fulfill my purpose in life. I always consider how every decision I make will affect your future. You are my reason for being strong, staying focused, and striving for success. We will make it, we will thrive, for we are, More Than A Statistic! To my More Than A Statistic supporters, I love you all from the bottom of my heart! We are going global!

Contact Info:
Stephanie Motley
www.more-than-a-statistic.org
morethanastatistic@gmail.com
Facebook: http://www.facebook.com/snm2223
Twitter: @Ms_MTS_CEO
Phone: 434-429-7786

THREE

FATHER ME? A LESSON IN LOVE
Angela N. Parris

I can still remember the first time he walked into the pizza shop. *Samson*, I call him. He looked just the way I imagined the biblical Samson would look, tall and strong with curly jet-black hair. His skin was coffee brown and when he flashed a smile it was all I could do to not giggle and run away screaming. I was already convinced that I was in love. Only, I didn't really know what love was – the love God intended anyway. This was pure fascination. I still can't believe how little it took to impress a headstrong schoolgirl like me. It didn't matter that he didn't keep a steady job and even though he drove, I don't remember seeing a valid license. So what if I couldn't figure out where he really lived or why he was always leaving town for days at a time? Ok, so he never showed up on prom night and didn't always come back when he said he would. Those things didn't seem to matter enough to make me stop wanting to be with him. I still get sad sometimes about my ignorance and I pray often that my children will know just how precious they are and that God has a design for family that will satisfy them beyond their wildest dreams. I hope they will know that design early enough not to be won over by something that only looks like love. My journey as a teenage mother was not loaded with financial woes or abandonment issues. Instead, my challenges came through emotional trials and spiritual conflicts that only God could resolve, but it would take resilience on my part if I was ever going to get to the kind of love that was meant for me all along.

I grew up without my biological father. That didn't mean I never had father-like love in my life; it's just that when it came along, I didn't recognize it. Sadly, I would pass it over because it didn't come packaged the way I thought it should. In a house full of women, we all had our own way of emulating dad-like qualities for one another. Even though a woman can provide for a home, only a man can bring true manlike qualities to that home – something was missing but we were living like it wasn't. I've come to understand that without God's love as an example, any one of us might be living like we've got it, only we really don't. When *Samson* took an interest in me, he was seven years my senior and he must've known that it didn't take much to impress a teenage girl. I leapt without looking, right into the very thing I thought I couldn't get at home, fatherly love. I learned later that I had been searching for something that couldn't be found in a man who didn't know the love of God.

The morning my mother stopped me before I could get down the steps for school, she was so calm. "You haven't gotten your period yet, have you?"

I swallowed hard. Of course I realized I was *late*, but I sure wasn't going to tell her and I had already convinced myself that pregnancy was not an option.

"Hmm, why do you ask?" I answered, trying to hide my nervousness. My mom had already counted the sanitary napkins in the bathroom. She was the sole income for the household and she had a mental inventory on everything that came and left those cabinets.

Her next words would change my life forever – "I'll make an appointment for the doctor today."

When the doctor's assistant came out with the positive test unit, it felt like a sea of hot water was rising up over my throat and ears. I expected to pass out at any moment. In fact, I was so scared, I wished I could make myself pass out, but it never happened. When I finally looked at my mom, she was slightly smiling at me through watery eyes. I was so confused.

She held my hand and said, "We're going to have a little nugget," or something like that.

Almost immediately, I blacked out mentally for what seemed like days. I later learned that I was already nearly seven months along and I couldn't believe this was really happening to me. I was determined to deny this pregnancy away.

I was the only girl in my entire high school to be visibly pregnant and to stay enrolled through graduation; not something I was proud of. Oddly enough, most people were amused and excited for me. Maybe they were trying to not hurt my feelings. I kept thinking, *When is someone going to tell me what a stupid mistake I have made?*

I had two baby showers, one by my family and one by my friends. I had so many gifts and surprises I began to think I had done something wonderful and maybe it wouldn't be so bad after all. My friends were onboard, my family was onboard, and so what if I couldn't tell where Samson really stood? All I had to do was graduate and start my new life as a parent, right? Nope.

In the weeks that followed, I felt like some sort of novelty in a sideshow. Friends and schoolmates were fascinated with my new little bump. It even amused me. Sometimes I'd walk slowly with my back slightly turned and then whip around to flash my belly and watch for their reaction. I still wanted someone to tell me how wrong this was, but they never did. It all seemed like a strange dream. That is, until the colleges stopped returning my calls.

I can still remember the awkward phone silence after each conversation with an admissions officer. They didn't even bother to make up a creative sorry like, "We don't have a daycare. (pause) Good luck then." Or, "Oh, well give us a call when your life comes back together."

It felt like I had never mattered in the first place. This was the wakeup call I had been looking for all along. I began to feel sick. All those years of marketing and fashion competitions down the drain. The endless hours my mom had devoted to supporting my dreams would end suddenly with no great accomplishment. Was *Samson* going to be around with a vision for our family? It was then that I decided to abandon all of my hopes and dreams that had carried me through high school and accept a life without a college degree, caring for my son, would be the best that I could expect. I prayed and cried often, but I didn't really pay attention to God. It's like I talked to Him, but never really looked for Him to talk to me.

On April 22, 1990, my little Mookie was born. *Samson* was there, and so were all of our family members. There were more balloons and gifts than I could carry home. In the months that followed, his family and my family seemed to be in some sort of unspoken competition over who could do the most for the baby. It was just weird. I was still beating myself up for becoming pregnant and everyone around me seemed to be celebrating. This journey was getting stranger each day. Life around me was falling into place, more or less. But something on the inside of me was slowly weakening and I couldn't even put my finger on it. So I did what I knew to get through each day and I went on as if nothing were wrong.

As a teen mother, I don't believe I struggled any more than anyone else who raises a child while trying to figure out her own childhood transitions. At the time Mookie was born, the cost for a low-income family to raise a child was around $107,000 per year.[i] I was making $18,200 and I didn't know much about managing money. I had no plan for how to build towards our future and I was learning everything as I went along. *Samson* would come around from time to time with a package of diapers, a new outfit or a few dollars, but it was never enough to cover the necessities. We did well most of the time. We did experience brief homelessness. It wasn't easy finding a place to stay on a limited budget and a woman can't legally share a bedroom with a male child, so one-bedroom or studio apartments were out of the question. I regularly waited for the bus with ten to fifteen shopping bags while toting a stroller, a baby bag on one shoulder, and Mookie on my hip. I was determined not to become a statistic but one year later, I was pregnant again. The child miscarried and I was disappointed in myself and in the fact that things weren't going as I had hoped. *Samson* was inconsistent. I was never a child support chaser. I just found it was easier to do what was needed, than to try and force the hand of someone who didn't care enough to overcome whatever obstacles stood in his way. If and when he made contributions, I called those unexpected surprises. That was better than feeling disappointed. If anything was necessary, it was up to me to make it happen.

When Mookie was about six years old, we were living in Philadelphia. One afternoon, I went to my Aunt's to pick him up and was stopped at the door. She told me some crazy story about why I couldn't come in and said I should come back later. I don't remember all the details. After a strange and heated exchange, I showed up later with a law officer. My mother met me at the door with court papers naming her as custodian and said I wouldn't be picking him up at all. How does that even happen? In my entire life, this season was about to produce the greatest lesson in forgiveness that I ever had to learn.

For months I worked, attended church and partied like life was cool. Yes, partied. Remember, I was still immature and I had convinced myself that because of what I was going through, I deserved to party. So I went along like everything was normal, only midway through the week, I'd get on a train and meet my mother at the Trenton train station to pick Mookie up for *my turn*. I would take him to daycare and play at home with him. Mookie loved visiting the Philly pier. From time to time his father would come to visit. On Sundays though, I'd meet my mother at another train station after church and hand him off. I lived with my best friend. She traveled with us each time and comforted me afterwards when I'd simply cry for days on end. I don't know how she managed to be in my life at that time. I tried to maintain some sense of normalcy, but all the while something deep inside of me was dying. My own mother was battling me for custody of my son; the father of my child remained aloof and uncommitted to our family; and each day the sun would rise and set and people all around me lived like everything was ok. *Today doesn't define tomorrow*, I kept telling myself.

I eventually regained full custody of Mookie and moved back to New Jersey. A girlfriend was going south and asked if I wanted to road-trip with her. I took her up and we hit the road for Charlotte, North Carolina, where life took a turn for the better. *Samson* had pretty much faded out of the picture except for his bi-annual call to get Mookie's hopes up only to let him down once more. Once, when he was about six or seven, Mookie begged to check the mailbox each day for over a month because he was looking for the birthday card and the Transformer that his father had promised, but they never came. I even gave him his own key so he could do it himself. The day he decided not to go back to the mailbox crushed my heart. I remember asking, "Will anyone ever father my child?" A change was coming, but at the time I could only see the same things happening around me.

A few years later, I met my husband. He's the most amazing person I have ever known. It hasn't been easy for him to build a family with us. We didn't have baby-daddy drama, but the road hasn't been without its bumps. Mookie still has the DNA of his biological father. He looks like him and has his sense of humor. More beautiful to me is how much of my husband's qualities he has adopted. The man he is becoming is heavily influenced by the man in his life today. There are endless books about the challenges of blended families and step-parent/child relationships. Our story is no exception. Our young children have never seen some of the things that Mookie has seen. He and I alone will adore and detest those seasons riding the city bus to go grocery shopping. He may not remember sleeping in a car or bathing in a public bathroom, because he was so young. But his life shows evidence of those hardships and I pray all the time that God will go easy on him and bring him to a beautiful place in life, as he has done for me. In my youth, I never thought that I'd be dealing with the remnants of my actions more than twenty years later. Forgiveness happened and it healed me, but it didn't mean that others weren't affected by those actions.

Speaking of forgiveness, I also forgave my mother for what happened all those years ago. I experienced the freedom that comes from true forgiveness and was able to be there for her later in life when she was facing a life transition. Today my mom lives nearby and is such a vital part of our lives. Our relationship is reconciled by God and all of my children enjoy having her around. I, too, love and adore her and realize that she made the best decisions she could with the knowledge and experience that she had. I guess that's what I am still doing today.

Making ends meet never scared me. My mother taught me to work and be resourceful by my own legitimate efforts. Any fool can do that if she believes she should. It was hard, but I believe sometimes you just have to put on your big girl panties and deal with it. Today, there are still times when Mookie wonders if his father will return his call. This is the heartache of a teen mother that cannot be known in your teenage years but shows itself much later in life. The hurt in my husband's eyes when Mookie withdraws because, "You're not my real dad," wasn't imagined in my teenage years. It was my thoughtlessness about how having a baby would affect others that still scares me sometimes. Once in awhile someone will ask, "If you had to do over again, would you?" Sure, but if I wouldn't do it differently, then I haven't learned anything. I would've paid better attention to the cues that *Samson* displayed early in our relationship. I would've tried to understand how my being so young and having a baby really affected *Samson* or my mother. I would've treasured my body more and drawn the line at no sex until I learned what true love is, so that I would know it when I had it. But Mookie? I wouldn't change a hair on his silky black head.

I still have one question: Did everyone *but me* know that God had a design for family that guarantees fulfillment if you follow the rules? My best friend tried to tell me about it a few times before I got pregnant, but I never paid it much attention. I always believed that God wanted me to have a good life, but I didn't understand that He had a roadmap for making that happen. This journey was hard and filled with crying days, but, because of it, I decided to learn about God's love. I wanted real love for Mookie and for myself. Today, I am blissfully married and our children have the funniest, most loving older brother they could ever want. They all have a father who loves God and loves them very much. Oh, my husband's smile makes me giggle and melt too; difference is, I'm no longer melting with fascination. This time it's really love and that lasts forever!

Love is patient, love is kind. It does not envy, it does not boast, it is not proud. It does not dishonor others, it is not self-seeking, it is not easily angered, it keeps no record of wrongs. Love does not delight in evil but rejoices with the truth. It always protects, always trusts, always hopes, always perseveres. Love never fails.
(I Cor. 13:4-8a, NIV)

[1] Lino, Mark. April 1996. *Expenditures on Children by Families*, 1995 Annual Report. U.S. Department of Agriculture, (Center for Nutrition Policy and Promotion, Washington, D.C.) Publication No. 1528-1995.

Author's Corner

Biography: Angela is a spirited wife of nearly 15 years to her dear husband and a joyful mother to six children. A journey in progress, her career has taken her from humble beginnings to high-powered board rooms –all without a college degree. Her life story bears proof of God's presence in all places. A mother at age 17, she never imagined she would one day enjoy a satisfying stable life as a married woman. Today Angela is a passionate orator who enjoys writing and serving in her home, church and community.

Acknowledgments: Praise God, the true author of my life! To my husband, you are I Corinthians 13 in hi-definition and I absolutely adore you. To the most amazing kids, I promise you an autograph if you promise one to me! Maahhhh, pray first then read 'k? Salad M and I are so blessed to have this new life with you! To Facie and the young ladies who held me up at Ewing High School, you were there for me in the moments that aren't told here; my life thanks God for you. To the seed, thank you for planting; I always wanted to make a garden grow. And most of all to Mookie, Psalms 139:13-14. Bologna, cheese and ketchup sandwiches for life!

Contact Info:
Angela Parris
mznikkiparris@aol.com
Facebook: https://www.facebook.com/mznikkiparris

FOUR

HEARD BY NO ONE
Sarah-Elizabeth Pilato

Don't have sex before you're married. That was the message. And this is my story.

I grew up in a supportive, well-rounded, two-parent Catholic home in the suburbs where I attended schools noted for academic excellence and performed many of the lead roles in the school plays and musicals. I was well-liked and respected by both my teachers and peers. I liked it that way, and made a concerted effort to ensure that it stayed like that. I grew up in a home rooted in faith, hope and love. It was a comfortable life. While all families share good times and bad times, I am convinced that our deep roots in faith, hope, and love were the key to our family's preservation. Like so many things we take for granted as children, my comfortable life in the suburbs was one of them. I remember having moments during my childhood when I wondered if it would ever get harder, more complicated, more challenging for me, or if this was really how my life was destined to be: easy. When exactly would I find out? Soon enough.

Nourishing our family was my mother- the strongest woman I know. She's a fighter. She will fight until the end if it means standing up for what she believes in. Although, during my late teen years I felt that her strong-will and strength of character challenged my new search for independence. It frustrated me more than anything else and I think the challenge scared her. Watching my mom interact with her friends and hearing her conversations with them on our old phone that sat in the kitchen connected to the wall so that everyone else in the house could hear your conversation, I understood that her loyalty to her friends and family ran deep. It is from my mother that I learned the value of food beyond physical nourishment. It also nourishes the soul. My mother was, and still is, a master at tastefully providing food as a token of her love. When my brother and I would return from college, there were always large home cooked meals waiting for us. When I would later have a miscarriage at the age of 27, she would come running out of her house towards our car with a box of frozen cheesecake and other various frozen desserts. I felt loved, and it felt right. It felt like the next best thing to a hug. However, like the comfort of my happy home in the suburbs, I wouldn't realize this for many years to come. In the meantime, she nourished my soul, and I ate. Unbeknownst to me, her food was turning me into the same strong, loyal, and faith-filled woman that she was. I didn't realize it at the time, but it wouldn't be long before I would need my strength. All of it.

While both of my parents contributed equally to my strong faith in God, they each had very different approaches. My father, the quieter, more laid back of the two, usually watched from the sidelines. But if you really knew my father, as I got to know him from tagging along with him for years, you would know that his peaceful silence really meant he was in the middle of saying a rosary for you or making a request to the saints for you. While this was also commonly done by my mother, (my mother was notorious for saying a rosary for people when they traveled, including the pilot), it was in the midst of my father's quietness, that I discovered my voice. I learned the value of a good conversation with God, and that there was nothing wrong with asking Him for a little help every once in a while. There were times that I remember my father being upset, or frustrated, or stressed, and whom did he turn to? God. He never complained about life. He took life as it was given to him, and asked God to help him through it. He always made it through. He had such faith. I wanted to know what that felt like. I yearned to be able to have that same relationship with God. My relationship with God was good, I had no problems. I think I was around 17 years old when I began to realize that maybe my life was not destined to be easy after all. Decisions started to get harder, and conversations with God became more frequent. I wasn't sure where my relationship with God was headed, but I did feel confident with one thing: my parents had prepared me for whatever was to come. I had this nagging feeling that there was something life-changing around the corner, something I would have to face alone. It was an uncomfortable feeling that I was destined for something unknown and I wasn't sure if it was good. I was young, and it wouldn't be until I was 19 years old that I would come face to face with that "something." And I would be right: it would be life-changing and I would face most of it alone.

I have always been a rule-follower. House rules, school rules, religious rules. You follow the rules and good things happen. Rules provided me with a feeling of gratification. The only rules I struggled with were the rules where I didn't see any sort of short-term gratification. If a rule wasn't going to benefit me immediately, it was more difficult for me to accept or follow. There was a darker side to following rules: temptation. It would be my worst enemy. Don't have sex before you're married. This rule I just could not follow. I tried, but I struggled to understand the harm in having sex, after all, who would know? I would. And it ate me up inside. I would talk to God about this. Did He understand my conflict? I thought so, but it was God! Even though I felt like He understood, I thought I should still try to follow the rules, right? So I did. I tried. I really did. And I was the only one who really knew. Right up until I couldn't hide it anymore. I had to have been around 4 months pregnant.

My grandfather (my mother's father) was dying and my parents were taking turns driving over to Buffalo to stay with him for days at a time. I loved my grandfather. We had the same blue eyes and shared the same love for the finer things in life, like over easy eggs and salami sandwiches. While he was sick, my parents sacrificed their social life with friends and their own relationship to be with him. As the eldest of three girls, and with my grandmother already gone, everything fell on my mother's shoulders. Some time to tell my mom and my dad that their only daughter was pregnant with their first grandchild by a boyfriend they hated. If only I had followed the rules.

In the months to follow, my heartbroken parents would attempt to support me the best way that they knew how, my boyfriend would try to encourage me to claim my independence from my parents, and my belly would continue to grow. I would move out of my parent's home to move in with my boyfriend and I would take a year off from college. I would give birth to my son and 4 days later my grandfather would pass away. I would miss him, and I would cry, but I would not grieve. My personal right to grieve was stolen from me by my boyfriend who refused to allow me to go to the cemetery for fear that my family would get our newborn sick. This wasn't the only moment he stole from me. He stole two years of my life! When I should have been studying at college, eating bad cafeteria food, decorating my dorm room, and going to bars with my girlfriends, I was scraping up pennies to buy groceries and crying myself to sleep.

I began my journey into motherhood alone. Although the hospital was full of friends and family on the cold December day that my son was born, no one knew how unhappy I was. Everyone would get a cute photo of the baby and leave. My friends would drive back to college and graduate in the spring. My family would resume their everyday lives. My boyfriend would escape to a world of chronic marijuana abuse, and would leave me tired, scared, broke, and dangerously thin. Do not have sex before you're married. It was all starting to sink in.

The first time I realized how alone I felt was when a nurse in the hospital picked Noah up out of the crib on wheels, handed him over to me on the hospital bed, and informed me that she'd be back in a little bit with some Ibuprofen. She told me she was going to give me some quiet time to be alone with my new baby. I sat up in the bed and bent me knees up towards my chest. I rested Noah's head against my legs and starred into his little blue eyes that were looking back at me. I think I muttered something like, "Hi, Noah. I'm your mom. I love you...". And then the tears started rolling down my cheeks. I realized I *was* his mom, and I didn't have a clue what I was doing. There he was. This precious little gift from God just looking up at me waiting for me to make my next move. There I was. This young girl, just looking down at him, waiting for him to make his next move. And that was how it would be for the next couple of years. We would help each other figure it all out. But in that moment, we came to an agreement that we didn't need to make a move; looking at each other was going to be just fine for now. I heard a soft knock at the door. The nurse asked me if I was OK. I forced a smile and told her that I was fine and that it was just my first moment alone with him that made me emotional. I told her I was overcome with joy. That was a lie. I was terrified.

And the terror would continue. Every night when Noah would wake up crying my heart would jump out of my chest and I would run into his room before his father would wake up. I had to get there quickly. If I didn't get there quickly enough, his father would wake up and there was no telling what he would do. Sometimes, he would wake up angry, swearing loudly about how he was tired and losing sleep. Sometimes, he would scream at Noah from bed to stop him from crying. I would thrust into survival mode. Sometimes, he would yell at me for not waking up quickly enough and for ruining his sleep because I let Noah cry for too long. Sometimes, I would not get there quickly enough and he would wake up first. That was never good.

By the time I woke up to Noah's cries, Frank was missing from bed. He was already in Noah's bedroom. My heart was racing as I ran towards the sound of his cries. When I got to the door, Frank shouted that he had it under control. I asked him if he needed any help and he asked me why I thought he needed help. I told him I didn't (lie #1), but was only offering to be nice (lie #2). He picked Noah up off the changing table and put him in his arms, attempting to soothe him. Noah continued to scream. Frank put him back on the changing table. I entered his room and picked Noah up off the changing table and offered to try rocking him to sleep. As I held Noah in my arms and began to walk out of his room, Frank approached me from behind and told me that he could do it himself. I turned around with Noah in my arms and told him that it was no big deal for me to take over for a little bit. As he got closer to us, it wasn't until I felt the palm of his hand hit my upper chest causing me to land hard against the wall behind me, that I realized the amount of rage that he had built up in those moments during which he had gotten to Noah before me. I stood there pressed against the wall with Noah in my arms thinking to myself that he had just crossed the line. I wanted to scream, and I wanted to cry. I wanted to fall to my knees and wake up from this horrible dream. *Please let me just go back to college and have fun. I had been raised by the strongest woman I knew, and the most faith-filled man I had ever met. How did I end up against a wall?*

I wouldn't tell anyone about what had happened. I was going to school to be a social worker. Social workers don't end up against walls. I felt like I needed to go on living my life as if everything was OK. I would put on a smile at work and serve coffee to strangers who would have no idea how miserable I was. I loved my son, but raising him alone wasn't easy. Customers would ask me about his father and I would have to make up excuses and lies about how great he was with Noah. I would leave out the parts about going into work without having slept for more than 15 minutes because I needed to make sure he didn't cry in the night and wake up his father. I left out the parts about having to work more shifts in order to pay our rent because Frank spent most of his paychecks on pot. I failed to mention that after paying the rent we had no money left for food and was mostly living off of leftover oyster crackers from restaurants and whatever drinks I made myself during my shifts. Looking back, I was lucky that I was able to breastfeed because there would have been no way we could have afforded formula. I left all of this out. I didn't want anyone to know, especially my parents.

It continued to get worse. The disappointment I had in myself constantly ate away at me. *I was supposed to be graduating from college and applying to grad schools, not living in poverty with an abusive boyfriend who couldn't control his anger around our helpless new baby.* I remember thinking this as he stood screaming at us from the living room. I don't even remember why he was angry, only that he was angry. I held Noah tight, he held me tighter. I was not going to let go; I was all he had. The pressure and the will to survive were overwhelming and the room was spinning. The rage in Frank's voice only made Noah scream louder, making Frank angrier. My thoughts were racing. *How bad was this going to get? Protect Noah*, I thought. We stood in the kitchen facing Frank as he screamed at us from the living room. Which, in the tiny apartment we lived in, was only about 10 feet away. We held onto each other for dear life as I calculated our next move. We stood in between the stove and side door to our apartment. The screaming continued and I wondered if I would find safety on the other side of that door. My grip around Noah became tighter as I gently rocked him up and down with the hope of convincing him that he was safe. More screaming. As we stood there holding each other through the cloud of rage that was quickly suffocating us, I remember my mouth moving, and words coming out, but I don't remember what I said. It's easy to forget things that you don't mean. When you're trying to survive, truth doesn't matter. All I had to do was reach my hand down, over that door knob and twist. *But then what? Who would save us?* More screaming. More lies. I was scared and panicking. *Please God*, I thought to myself, *please make this OK*. I didn't even know what to ask Him for; I just needed it to stop. He stormed into the kitchen, a couple feet away from us and we stepped back. He stepped closer. More screaming. At that moment, I felt a burst of strength and blurted out that we were going to walk out that door. That was it; he didn't want to lose us. Losing us meant losing control. Silence. *Was I really going to leave?* We stood there paralyzed in silence, and that's all I remember. It got quiet and we were OK. *Thank you God*.

I knew it wasn't right. The entire thing was completely wrong. He was wrong for me, I was wrong for him. Having sex before I was married was wrong. Moving in with him was wrong. Enduring his abuse was wrong. I was 19 years old, and not at all who I thought I was. I thought I was strong and faith-filled. Yet, there I was rotting away in my soul. He tried to convince me that he should go to college and get his degree first (in what, he had no clue) since he was both older and the man in the relationship. Was he really asking me to forfeit my education and career? Yes. I didn't know how much longer I could endure this. My best friend from high school abandoned me as if being pregnant was a contagious disease. My two other high school friends tried to help, but they had lives of their own. And again, they wouldn't have known how badly I needed them—my screams for help were silent and heard by no one. My parents tried to support me and constantly encouraged me to return to college, but I felt like God was the only one who really heard me. He heard me, but I did not hear Him. I was so consumed in my chaos that I forgot to listen. Sometimes you really are your own worst enemy.

While my pain was silently swallowed up in tears, Frank's yelling continued to grow louder. This time, I stood in the living room, feeling the all too familiar desperation of a mother lion whose cub had just been taken from her. *Give-me-my-baby.* Every time Frank screamed, Noah screamed. Every time Noah screamed, Frank yelled louder. Frank had unsuccessfully been trying to get Noah to stop crying. My offer to help turned into a rage of how I must think he is a bad father. I made multiple attempts to approach him, each greeted with more anger and more screaming. I just wanted to hold my baby. I couldn't get to him. I was desperate. *Please don't shake him,* I thought. I had to be careful. It wasn't as simple as just going over to him and taking the baby. This was life or death. If I made the wrong move there was no telling what he would do next. He had my baby. I needed to protect my baby. And then it occurred to me, whether he was hungry or not, I'd make Frank believe that Noah needed to be breastfed. And that was how I got my baby back. Thank God again for breastfeeding! Noah stopped crying immediately and latched on for comfort as if his life depended on it. I sat there holding his warm little body close to mine, feeling his little heartbeat racing in time with mine, and I wept silently. I should have been in class.

I felt like I was wasting away both mentally and physically. My parents kept questioning me about returning to college. I felt the pressure and knew I had to make my move. If I had stayed in college, I would have already had my master's degree by now. But I had to let that go. I had to live in the present and take it for what it was. Returning to college as a mother was God's plan for me and I was going to embrace it.

Stepping back on a campus was so refreshing. I felt at home, and I felt a new sense of hope. The people at this new school prayed for each other before class, cared about your day, brought out the goodness in others, and everyone wanted you to succeed. I needed those things back in my life. I was finally in the right place at the right time. I felt closer to God more than I had ever felt before. I met three amazing women the year I returned to college. They didn't judge me. They didn't advise me. They listened to me. They loved me. It was because of them that I learned to listen back, and, eventually, I began to hear God again. I began to hear Him everywhere I went.

He wasn't telling me to turn my life around, He was telling me to turn around and run for my life. I dropped Noah off at my parent's house one night, had a couple of my friends on call in case I needed help, and went over to the apartment to tell Frank it was over. I sat on the brick steps with him as he cried and begged me to stay. At that moment, I was speechless. All I knew was that I needed to tap into my reserve of strength-the strength stored up from the unconditional love and spiritual nourishment from my parents. I had to leave. I asked God to give me the words that I needed. I couldn't tell you what I said, but somehow the words came out. They weren't mine, they were God's.

Noah and I moved into my brother's old bedroom and my parents watched Noah while I went to class and worked. I would leave for class before he woke up in the morning and return from work after he had fallen asleep for the night. There were some days that I only saw him for 15 minutes. But those 15 minutes were not filled with screaming or tears and I hoped that he would someday understand that it was worth it. I was more alive than I had been in years.

In between classes and work, I somehow stumbled upon love. I promptly informed this new love interest that Noah and my education were my number one priority and that the only available time I had to go out on a date with him was Saturday morning at 4:00am and that I had to be back by 9:00am to go to work. I was in a committed long-term relationship with God, and Noah. Anyone interested in me would have to understand that. And he did. That Saturday we went out for breakfast and bought empanadas at the public market. For the first time in my life, I felt what it was like for someone other than my own parents to love me unconditionally, regardless of my imperfect past. And better yet, he loved my son, too. I didn't expect anyone to be able to break down the walls I had built around myself and Noah, but he did. And that's where faith came in. All things are possible through Him.

I went on to marry the man of my dreams, and to obtain my bachelor's degree in social work and my master's degree in social work with a concentration in child and family services. I vowed to myself that I would commit my life to helping young girls and women of all ages to not only choose life for their babies, but to choose life for themselves as well. It is possible to have both. Following graduation, I became the associate director of a pregnancy center offering both counseling and material assistance for women in need. There, I met many young girls like myself. They reminded me of that young girl who came home from college one summer and hid her belly from her parents. I later became a supervisor at a local community agency, where services are provided to parents and families who are identified as being at risk for foster care, abuse or neglect.

My life is committed to helping people find strength during times of weakness and hope during times of loss. My parents prepared me well for my journey, and, now, I prepare others for theirs. Our stories are our own and the ending is up to us.

Don't have sex before you're married was the message. Resilience is my story.

Author's Corner

Biography: Sarah-Elizabeth Pilato, LMSW, holds a bachelors in social work and a masters in social work with a concentration in child and family services. Sarah-Elizabeth is married to her loving husband Brian, and is the proud mother of Noah and Ava.

Acknowledgments: To God, my provider and my strength. To Mary, Mother of us all, for taking on the role of mother at such a young age and modeling true faith and strength through which you give us comfort and hope to overcome all doubts, fears, and difficulties that come with unplanned motherhood. To my husband, for loving me, and always believing in me and pushing me to follow my dreams. To my parents, for teaching me that your passion and purpose in life cannot be taken away from you, no matter how great the obstacle, as long as true strength grows within you out of faith and trust in God. To my brother, always ready to shed light on new perspectives and opportunities. To my children, Noah and Ava, for their unconditional love and for reminding me daily about the important things in life. To LaShunda, for inspiring me to be passionate about my work by doing what I love and loving what I do. To everyone in my story who believed in me. Thank you.

Contact Info:
Sarah-Elizabeth Pilato, LMSW
www.sarahelizabethpilato.com
sarahepilato@gmail.com
Facebook: https://www.facebook.com/S.E.Pilato
Twitter: @sarahepilato
LinkedIn: Sarah-Elizabeth Pilato, LMSW

FIVE

AMBITIONS OF A BLACK PEARL
Tanishia A. Johnson

For a moment, in silence, close your eyes. Go to the most quiet and peaceful inner part of your being. Reflect on your life when you were 7, 8 or 9, when you knew what you wanted to be when you grew up. Think about why you decided that *this* was what you wanted to be. Think about the moment you decided that *this* was what you wanted to do forever. How badly did you desire being that doctor, lawyer, dancer, actor or teacher? How much did you want the thing that made you happy at the first thought of it? Now I want you to go to the moment in which you realized that all you had hoped for, dreamed about and desired would be harder than you thought, maybe even something you could not accomplish. How much did your heart sink in that moment?

In the beginning, I, like many of you, had dreams and hopes of being something great. I desperately wanted to help people. A Catholic school girl, raised in the South Bronx in the 80's, I knew I was going to be a nun or pediatrician. From as far back as I can remember, I wanted to be liked. No. I wanted to be loved, accepted and seen as perfect. When I was younger, the greatest examples of that to me were nuns. I always thought that I had a "special" relationship with God and I wanted to do everything to please Him. I also remember the moment I wanted to be a pediatrician. I loved babies; I loved anything that had to do with loving a baby. I was fascinated by the way pediatricians worked with young patients and I visualized myself being called "Dr. Chandler" someday. Add to this, I loved my pediatrician. She was caring and always seemed interested in me, as a person. Yes. I knew I was going to be a pediatrician and a nun. But then it happened. I remember the very moment it occurred to me: this may not be a possibility. I remember thinking there was no way I could reach these goals because I wasn't good enough, talented enough, or smart enough. I was about 10 when I stopped liking what I saw in the mirror. The words of my grandmother finally broke me, the lack of response from my mother hurt me and the absence of my father's love, nearly destroyed me.

Broken

I was the child expected to do everything right. The second child with none of the challenges my older sister, who struggled academically, had. My nose was always in the books. I often thought about what it would feel like to know that I was the one that everyone in the family adored. I was my mother's darkest child and from as far back as I can remember, I was always negatively reminded about this by a grandmother who was as dark as me. "Blackie," or, "Black B****", stop smiling with your black gums," or, "Quit laughing like a black cheesy cat," is often what I heard.

I was 10 or 11 when I would smile without showing my teeth. Often, I felt very uncomfortable when I did smile; thinking everyone else thought my smile was ugly because of my "black gums." I never heard my mom defend me or stand up to my grandmother who lived with us throughout my childhood. My mother's silence, at that time, meant some of what grandma said to me, about me, had to be true.

My father, still married to my mother, was away on duty throughout my childhood. He was a navy man and I was so proud of that in my early years. As time went on, I began looking for him at school events with promises from my mother that he would be at my kindergarten graduation, 1st Holy Communion, birthdays, holidays, etc. Instead, he would write letters from time to time, most of which were addressed to my older sister. I envied my older sister because I felt she was favored. He would send gifts to her "just because", while I received a letter composed of his recent travels. My sister's skin was lighter than mine and her hair was fuller and straighter and this was something family constantly made reference to, when comparing us. My older sister was the apple of my father's eye, as the family put it.

My grandmother had talks with her that she never had with me. I remember watching from the distance, the times she would pull her close and the smile my older sister would put on Grandma's face. I began feeling insecure about everything. For years, I hated my middle name because my mother gave me Grandma's name. I hated my nappy hair, which she always talked about. My black gums, my smile, the dark pigment of my skin, I hated them all. I remember sneaking products in to see if the color of my face or arms could change by using them. Bleached smelling hands, Ambi cream in our bathroom cabinet—I tried it all. I wanted desperately to be light-skinned and I began noticing that all of the boys were giving more attention to the lighter skinned girls. Why was I so damn black and ugly?!

I resented what I saw in the mirror and by the time I was 12, although I still wanted to be "something" when I grew up, I knew that being a nun or pediatrician probably wasn't it. My grandmother would say that I would need to be with a lighter man someday because of how "black" I was and that I would have babies "dark as night" (as if this were a bad thing). My family would sometimes make a fuss if I were in the sun because they said I would just get darker. And there was always this talk about putting certain colors on me—colors too bright may not look good against my skin. I will never forget someone saying to my grandmother, in reference to dark skin, "The blacker the berry, the sweeter the juice."

My grandmother returned without batting an eye, and with me in her view, "But if you get them any blacker, they ain't no damn use."

Memories of my father coming home, barely once a year, began to be what I held onto. When he did come home, there was a lot of attention given to my older sister. I would watch and ask myself, "Why doesn't he love me the way he loves her?" "Why doesn't he hold me, the way he holds her or speak to me the way he speaks to her?" It was as if he *loved* her and *tolerated* me. I began resenting my older sister and our relationship was hindered because when we did argue or disagree, I was usually the one considered wrong and was told, "Shut your black _____ up."

I hated being hit in the face, smacked in the mouth and verbally disrespected, but in our home, *you stayed in a child's place.* There were times I never understood the reasons behind my mother's and grandmother's whippings and other times I thought that my grandmother would whip me because she just didn't like me. She often rolled her eyes at me or looked at me with disgust or would just shake her head as if there were something shameful about me. My 13th birthday came, and I remember thinking that I could not wait to grow up, get out of this house and be on my own, away from it all. Then I turned 14 and *he* walked into my life and I fell in love. Broken, but desperately in love.

I Said YES

Nico was beautiful, in my eyes. He was tall, light skinned, slim, and everything I thought I wanted in a first boyfriend. I was 14 when we met, he was 18. I was in love with him; I physically ached at the thought of him not wanting to be with me. He was from a broken home and his mother was an addict. He never knew his father and was raised in the foster care system. Once he aged out, he lived with his grandmother whose project complex was in the back of mine. I remember the first time I saw him, sitting on the bench in the back of our connected buildings. It was the first time butterflies danced in my stomach. I was in love at first sight and knew that he would be "the one" always. He was kind, gentle, was cool with all the guys, and, of course, all the girls in the projects adored him. But, he paid attention, to me.

Almost immediately, we were dating and even with the red flags in the beginning, his disappearing acts, his flirtatious ways with other girls, etc., I was still Nico's girl and everyone knew it. I began to imagine my life with him; there was no way I could imagine life without him. Nico began having issues with his grandmother and my mother decided to move him in with us. At this point in my life, my mother gave birth to my younger sister, and, a few years later, my younger brother. She then decided to move on without their fathers. My dad was absent and unable to ever be reached. We relocated to a small town where my uncle lived. Of course, Nico followed us.

Our relationship became stronger and I began feeling as though no one else in the world but me mattered to him. I felt the same way about him. He was loving toward me; he talked about how beautiful my skin was to him. He would talk with me for hours, we shared stories of our lives and where we wanted to be years down the road. I felt beautiful with him. I felt like somebody with him and there was no denying the fact that I would do anything to stay in this relationship. He was my first love. We talked about having children. I remember when he proposed, asking me to be with him forever, to trust him and to know that anything that I ever wanted, he would provide. In my mind, we would be like my mother and father, who married as teens. I never looked at the fact that my mother was now alone and raising us on her own with my grandmother's support. I only saw what was right in front of me; a man that loved me. My first intimate moment with Nico was planned. I remember the moment I made up my mind that he was worthy of that precious part of me. In spite of the fact that he had already cheated on me, had left me for days or months at a time with no call, and had given poor explanations of his needing space, I decided that he was deserving of this part of me. This precious part of me that, once given away, I could never get back. That sacred part of me, my virginity. Yes, he was deserving. I never thought for a second that he wasn't. It made sense because he loved me more than I loved myself. Nico was older so of course thoughts of him with girls that were "ready" were always on my mind. I could not lose the one person who was my whole world. The one person I knew who loved me. The night I lost my virginity to Nico was the night I knew he would want me and love me forever. I never thought about my feelings about *it* happening. Only what this meant for my relationship with him. I never told my mother, but, deep down, she knew her little girl had lost her innocence.

Mom began to notice changes in me and she wanted Nico out of the house. I was determined to be with him, and weeks later, I found out that I was pregnant. This was not a shock, of course. We planned it. I was so empty inside that I felt a baby could fill my void and love me unconditionally. Scared, but excited, I told Nico I was pregnant with our love child, and, yes, he was happy. When my mother learned of my pregnancy, she was angry. I shared with her that I wanted this baby and she immediately called my father overseas to share this news. My father and I, at this point, had not spoken to each other in years. Surprisingly, he did not support my mother's desire to forbid me from moving forward with the pregnancy. At the same time, my father was not loving, barely reached out to me and was dismissive. But he was adamant.

"My daughter will not be going under the knife."

Nico left town at the start of my pregnancy and days later, I found myself heading back to New York City to be with him. My mother still maintained that I was not having this baby; but I was determined to have the one thing I felt I needed. I remember feeling so alone. I just wanted her to tell me that she loved me and that even though she did not agree with my decision, she still loved me. She didn't. I had no other support. We were in a new town and the adults that knew my mom supported her. I had one friend that showed concern for me, but, naturally, that wasn't enough. It was time for me to leave. I was already in love with this child growing inside of me. I didn't have a clue as to how I would do it but I knew that nothing would stop me from providing for this baby. I decided to say yes to having this baby, even if it meant that I would be on my own.

Moment of Truth

Days turned to months and I refused to contact my mother until I reached out to my father's mother, who told me that my mother was concerned. I decided, after speaking with her, that I would come back in an effort to rebuild our relationship. I knew my mother was disappointed in me and I knew she had every right to be. No parent wants to learn of her teenage daughter being pregnant. Nico came back with me and for the last few months leading up to and following our son's birth, things were difficult. I struggled to understand the changes taking place in my body and Nico struggled from one job to the next. I went on home instruction and stayed on track with school, determined not to drop out.

On April 24, 1990, at 7:24 p.m., Rafael Wendell Walker was born. I was unable to see him right way because of an 18-hour labor and an emergency C-Section. The moment I woke up and looked into his eyes, I knew nothing in the world mattered more than he. I wanted Rafael to have a wonderful life with married parents who loved each other and provided a great life for him. It all became real in that moment. Barely three months after Rafael was born, my mother pressed statutory rape charges against Nico. I moved out again. I supported Nico in court right up until he denied that he was Rafael's father. Hurt, confused, and with paternity test documents in hand, I left the courtroom. Nico knew he was the only man I had ever been with; his paternity denial hurt me to the core.

During this time, Nico also became abusive. He would leave the home for days at a time. Our arguments became so bad that when I tried to stop him from leaving me, he would push me, throw me down, or do whatever he had to do to leave us. And to add insult to injury, he became intentionally careless in his infidelity, further violating our relationship by having an affair, in our home, with a friend. In these moments, I thought about who I was as a person. I had never witnessed any woman in my family being abused. I came from a long line of alpha females and deep within me, I knew I wanted to get out before things got worse.

As court proceeded, my mother dropped the charges. The paternity results proved that Ralphy was Nico's son. As I left court, I realized that I deserved better. I knew that I could not keep a man that did not want to be kept, regardless of whether or not I had a child with him. I could not be with a man that openly denied his son in a courtroom full of people knowing that it was a lie. I wanted to be more than what I was and I accepted that Nico was not the man I fell in love with—he was the shadow of a man that I had created in my mind. My feelings of being in love were real, but I was in love with someone that didn't exist. I packed Ralphy up, moved in with a friend, worked evenings and went to school during the day.

My friend was part of a church whose pastor's wife helped babysit Ralphy. I ate at work many nights because of the shortage of food. Mother Avery must have known this because she would often give me groceries when I picked up Ralphy. I finally applied for WIC, Medicaid and food stamps which helped tremendously. I hated the way I was looked at in those appointments and the way I was treated. They even asked how and when Ralphy was conceived. There was no way I was staying on this system, although I needed it then. Ralphy had well child checks. Food was scarce, but I was not going to quit school to take on a 2nd job which would lessen my time with my baby boy. I never received a penny in child support because Nico was supposedly working under the table and he couldn't be located.

Although mom and I were speaking, I could not return to her home because of an ongoing investigation from a time when my mother struck me. I was officially on my own. I decided that

I would not be the statistic my school counselor pegged me to be. He had recommended trade schools instead of college, but I knew better and made a decision to get back to the basics of who I was. I decided it was time for me to work through some relational issues with my mom. When the investigation was closed, my mother and I worked on our issues. While my grandmother was still residing with mom, her health was failing and she did not concern herself with what was taking place with me, at all.

I decided to make a strong finish with high school, and, in my senior year, applied to colleges, received several small scholarships and graduated with grades I was proud of. With my "Ralphy" on my hip graduation day, I knew what I had to do. My mother and I had had several conversations about my joining the military even as I had college acceptances on the table. I wanted to provide for my son. As I got further into the process I thought of my relationship with my absent father and knew the military was not the direction for me to go in. I decided the gateway to a greater life for me and my son was college. I would be the first in my family, on both sides, to go to college and began thinking that I *could* do this. I did everything the financial aid Advisors instructed me to do.

It was decided after many talks with my mother that the best option for me was to attend Brockport College, away from home. There was a hole in my heart. I could not fathom a day without my baby. He and I had been on this ride together and his face, his smell, and our routine were the things that kept me going. I began thinking of what I didn't have and what I wanted for Ralphy. I thought about how much our family struggled. I literally envisioned Ralphy and me in a house, my working a career, and us taking on the world. I began understanding that I could make a difference for my family. I thought about my neighborhood and saw young girls with one or two babies. Many of these teen parents were on welfare, were dropouts, and had numerous baby daddies and so forth and so on. I couldn't go back to New York City as I had no relationship with my father or the relatives who lived there. I knew without a college education, attaining a better life would be a challenge. My mother assured me that leaving him in her care was the best option as Ralphy would not be uprooted and I could get my education. She understood that I wanted to and needed to be active in his life, especially as his mother and his financial provider. Ralphy was a little more than 3 when I left for college and there were many times I cried because I felt I could not physically be there if he needed me late at night, early in the morning, or even if he had had a bad day in school. I went back and forth, took trips home on the weekends as often as I could, went home for breaks, holidays, birthdays, and made numerous calls to find out about his day to day life. I worked two jobs to continue his support, sending or bringing home my pay checks and loan refunds to ensure that whatever he needed, he received. I wanted him in Catholic school and enrolled him, sending money to cover his tuition. His teachers knew how to contact me. My mother was phenomenal in keeping me in the loop about everything and his well-child doctor appointments were scheduled around times that I would be home. I never missed a major event and I balanced all of this while taking a full course load.

As time went on, I saw that Ralphy was continuing to thrive and as graduation neared, I grew more excited. I graduated with my bachelor' degree in psychology and stood proud with a few hundred other scholars who all had a different story to tell. Mine was one that was filled with all the growth, hard work and perseverance I had experienced over the years. I learned a great deal about myself through those years. During the times when Nico did try to come in and out of our lives, it became easier for me to resist going back to the person I once was. I was no longer a young and naïve, crazy in love teenager; I was a woman on a mission. Although I still struggled with low self-esteem, and had a couple of heartbreaks along the way, what became more important was the woman and mom I wanted to be and the mom that I wanted my son to look up to and to be proud of. I prayed to God constantly asking Him to lead me in a direction that would give me the ability to provide for my son and to be an outstanding mother. I knew upon leaving Brockport that it was time to get settled into a career that would take Ralphy and me to a different level. I was blessed to secure a full time job with benefits, a job that set the stage for where I am now. I moved into a stable apartment with my baby boy in tow. I was feeling as if I could take on the world.

The Rebirth of ME

I met my husband, Cory, weeks after college graduation, but in the beginning saw him only as a friend. He was a smooth dark skinned brother, who was the first man to look beyond who I was outwardly, and I fell in love with him. It was the first time that the words of my grandmother about dating "light men" faded away. Cory was different from any other man I had ever met. He was selfless, completely about my and Ralphy's needs. This love was mature, safe, responsible and life-giving. Cory was interested in me as a person, encouraged me, motivated me, and understood me. He was in love with Ralphy and immediately stepped into the role of dad. Ralphy was 7 at the time and guarded; the process took a while. Nico, at this point, had relocated and there was no contact with him for a few years, which made it even harder for Ralphy to trust Cory. Cory was patient. He ventured into Ralphy's world and really got to know him, understand him and love him. Ralphy finally let him in.

Cory and I began planning our lives together, envisioning what we wanted our future to be as a family. We began planning our wedding and having discussions about how our life would look after marriage. We attended Engaged Encounter and for the 18 months leading up to our wedding date we had counseling sessions with our pastor where we left no topic off the table. We married August 5, 2000, and four more beautiful children later, with close to 17 years in relationship, 13 in marital union, our life could not be fuller. During this time Cory also adopted Ralphy and the process we went through was a journey we will never forget. There were tears of joy in the judge's chambers, as this process was intense. Nico had to be given due notification and after many court dates where he never appeared, the judge finally granted the order stating that my husband was indeed already his father and no document could make that any clearer. Cory was legally named as Ralphy's father.

Through my husband's support and encouragement, I went to graduate school and completed my master's degree in education (counseling). I started the program in 2003, pregnant with our second to youngest child, and sat in the stands on graduation day in 2006, expecting our youngest child. It was the height of my life, and my proudest moment, as my family and children watched me get my degree. It was the most important moment in my life and my father and mother attended. It was the first time I saw my parents together, happy with, and for me in my adult life. It was also the first time that I thought my father and I would have a father/daughter relationship. Throughout all of this, I became actively involved in many organizations, giving back to the community. I was offered a position as school counselor prior to my completion of the program. This was my rebirth.

I was becoming the person I knew God destined me to be. I beat the odds and became the first in my family to not only hold a bachelor's and master's degree, but the first to own a home, to drive and own a car and as an adult, to not live on a system that tells me how to live or care for my family. My proudest accomplishment is that I am also the first in my family to be in a strong marital relationship where my husband and I are in love and are raising our children together.

While pursuing my graduate degree, I also sought counseling for much of the emotional baggage that I still carried. As I took more time to look in the mirror, I began to love the person I saw, and when negativity crept in, I stepped aside and allowed God to take over. It took a while for me to allow my husband to fully love me for the woman I was. I struggled with intimacy because of my feelings of insecurity. There were moments I doubted his love for me because I still didn't fully love myself.

Through his unconditional love, his prayers for and with me, and our involvement in marriage encounters, I was able to truly see him for the phenomenal husband and father he was; I am blessed to have him in my life. I was finally able to allow myself to be open and vulnerable, knowing that this love was real and powerful.

Forgiveness became a large part of my journey. I grew to understand that my parents and grandparents were not perfect and they did what they could based on their life experiences. I began to be more prayerful and thankful that I had the support to continue my education. I began to gain an understanding that all of the things I went through were a part of my testimony. A testimony I would share to help inspire others. When I think back on all of my experiences, I think of my resilience and my ability to keep moving forward in spite of life's obstacles. I feel pride as I reflect on how I was able to change the outcome of my family's legacy due to the positive decisions I made which impacted everyone around me. I have broken the generational curse of teen motherhood followed by a life in poverty and broken relationships.

Ralphy went to the best schools, received his Advanced Regents High School Diploma and is now attending college, pursuing a career as a writer and a dancer. We are so proud of him and he is just starting to set this world on fire. I believe that each generation is supposed to do better than the generation before it. I know my parents are proud of me. I know that my ancestors, whose struggles significantly outweighed mine, would be proud.

Beyond This Moment

At this moment in my life I am researching doctoral programs. I am launching my life coaching and motivational speaking business, continuing my work as a counselor and broadening my platform to service communities in need. My life's work is to inspire other women to pursue what they are being called to do. My other passion is working with teen moms and dads who need to know that being successful in terms of education, personal goals, achieving your dreams and doing what you are called to do on this earth, is not only possible, but completely attainable. My work with youth is important to me because there were not many people who encouraged me to go to college. I want to encourage as many young people as I can, letting them know that where you start is certainly not always where you end up.

I still have struggles. My relationship with my father being one example. We haven't spoken since he disowned me soon after my graduate ceremony, sending a message publicly via email to me and other family members that he no longer wanted to have anything to do with me. I have learned to love him at a distance and I no longer internalize how he treats me. I learned years ago that he struggles with alcoholism and that this is not something I can control. I can only control how I respond. It has taken many years for my mother and me to be more loving toward one another. My mother did the best she could with what she had. What touched me the most was the moment she apologized for all she had done to cause me pain and especially for all my grandmother had done to me. I also

70

asked for her forgiveness for the pain I had caused her, wanting her to know how much it meant to me that despite everything that had happened, she still supported me.

I now take accountability for the relationships I am in with people and work hard at those relationships that are life-giving to me and my family. I have built relationships with women who have continuously supported and inspired me. I make a greater effort to stay connected in those life-giving relationships. I now realize that much of my lack of deep personal relationships with women stem from some of the betrayals I have experienced. I am at a peaceful place amongst all the chaos of being a wife, mother, daughter, sister, counselor and friend. I love the life that God has blessed me with and I appreciate the struggles because today, it's my testimony. Beyond this moment, I am looking to channel all that I have learned into inspiring others. I have moments where I fall into patterns of insecurity and self-doubt, but the biggest difference for me today is that I now recognize the triggers that can cause me to self-destruct and I have the tools to defeat those moments: love and support from my family, inner strength, prayer and my relationship with God.

Laurore Jean Pierre wrote: *So beautiful and unique, such strength and only Faith stands by you. The tears that you cry fall into the ocean keeping others hoping, beautiful on the outside and amazingly gorgeous on the inside. Your pride of how you came about helps you fight words that are sharper than knives. You have been through hard times, but you survived because you are a BLACK PEARL. Waves might direct you but you lead your own destiny.*

Today, I am simply living each day as a gift that God has given me: honoring my past, enjoying my present, embracing the future...beyond this moment. I am looking to soar, flourish and inspire; leaving a mark on this world that all great things are possible through God. All of this through *His* grace and mercy and because of my journey.

Author's Corner

Biography: Tanishia Johnson is a passionate counselor, life coach and motivational speaker. She works professionally and privately as an advocate and social justice ambassador for youth. As a school counselor and a student and family support coordinator for the Rochester City School District, Tanishia is passionate about serving the youth and young adult population, specifically in urban settings. She holds a bachelors of science degree in psychology with a criminal justice minor. She also holds an M.S.Ed in Counseling, both from The College at Brockport. She is an active member of several professional counseling organizations. Mrs. Johnson is nationally certified as a disaster mental health counselor and is regionally certified as a community emergency response team member. A certified trained facilitator in Effective Black Parenting, she believes that parents are instrumental in the well-being of their child. A believer in restorative practices, building community and resolving conflict, she has been trained in Peace Circles and Restorative Justice Community Conferences. An active member of Zeta Phi Beta Sorority, Inc., she holds the position of 3rd Vice-President to the local Theta Alpha Zeta chapter in Rochester, New York. She is an active member as Elder DIVA of the City of Rochester Determined DIVAS Program, Education Co-Chair for the Education Committee of The Black Women's Leadership Forum, and is a commissioner for the Greater Rochester Rev. Dr. Martin Luther King, Jr. Commission. She is a group member of Sistahs on the Move, and a commissioner of the Diocese of Rochester-Black

Leadership Commission representing her church home, St. Ambrose/Peace of Christ. Her greatest pride and joy is her 13 year marriage to her loving and supportive husband Cory, and being mom to their 5 beautiful children: Rafael, Kyle, Jordyn, K'mari and Khairi.

Acknowledgments: First and Foremost, I would like to thank God, my creator and savior for Blessing with me all that He has given me and for placing important people in my life that stood in the gap in order for me to be successful. My journey, my story, my testimony is because my God has covered and anointed me and blessed me with those important people. To my husband, Cory, you are my hero, my backbone and my strength. Thank you for always encouraging me to do more and to do those things that I thought would only be a dream. I love you with every breath of my being. To my children, you are my inspiration and Joy. I dedicate this to you so that you may know that you can fulfill your dreams in spite of the setbacks and challenges that life throws your way. I love you all endlessly: Rafael, my first born by whom this story was brought to life, and Kyle, Jordyn, K'mari and Khairi. To my beloved mother, Hattie Chandler, I admire your strength and the love and support you have provided me. I know that as a teen mom yourself, raising us was not easy but you did the best you could with all you had. I love you and appreciate you tremendously. To my extended family, thank you for all of your love and support through the many paths life has taken me. To my Sorors, my BWLF sisters and to all those "special" women in my life who have supported me: I love you and from the bottom of my heart, I thank you for loving, supporting and embracing me. To LaShunda Leslie-Smith, thank you for inspiring me, for your remarkable vision and for providing a venue for my story to be told. To the contributing authors: Sisters, this has been a phenomenal journey that I will always treasure. You are all amazing, beautiful women and your stories will inspire many. I also dedicate the writings of my journey to all young moms including those whom I have encountered and have yet to encounter. Keep pushing and your amazing testimony will someday be revealed and will inspire others! God Bless you and your children.

Contact Info:
Tanishia Johnson
www.beyondthismoment.com
tanishia.johnson@gmail.com
Facebook: https://www.facebook.com/tanishia.johnson
Twitter: @BYondThisMoment
Linked In: Tanishia Johnson, MSEd.
Phone: 585-351-9016

SIX

CROWN OF BEAUTY
Elizabeth Reyes

...to bestow on them a crown of beauty instead of ashes, the oil of joy instead of mourning, and a garment of praise instead of a spirit of despair. They will be called oaks of righteousness, a planting of the Lord for the display of his splendor.
—Isaiah 61:3 (NIV)

Before I share my story I must say, God has done great things in the lives of my family over the last 27 years. He has redeemed us through His salvation and has given us a godly lineage after so many generations of godlessness. God has delivered us from generational curses that would have kept us bound and would have devastated our future. May my story serve as evidence of God's love and mercy.

In the Beginning

I remember living with my *mami* (mother), *abuela* (grandmother) and *titi* (aunt). The house was always full of kids, loved ones and friends. If ever my mother had to work, I still had two

76

wonderful ladies in my life to love and care for me and my little sister (my baby brother hadn't been born yet). I remember my family setting up a table on the sidewalk in front of the house and playing dominoes on a warm summer night. I remember the laughter, *la musica salsa* (salsa music), dancing and delicious food. I remember opening the fire hydrant on a hot summer day and using a can to direct the water. I remember how I didn't have a care in the world. I was 9. I was at peace. I was happy. That changed.

I remember my father coming home from prison and this happy reality quickly became a thing of the past. Now, my family was comprised of my father, mother, and younger sister and soon after, baby brother. With the addition of my father, and the exclusion of our extended family, we were now a very closed family. No friends came over to visit and my extended family would rather not know what was going on in my house.

What the Struggle Looked, Sounded and Felt Like

Most often, my father only spoke to us to reprimand or to belittle us. He was an authoritarian; he always had the last word. In my home, sometimes wrong was right and right was wrong and you never could tell. My father drowned his sorrows in alcohol and drugs which only numbed him to our cries for a father who would love, protect and provide for us (although he had his own way of displaying these attributes). As a child, I viewed my mother as a saint sent from heaven to love and protect me the best she knew how. She had me at a young age, 15. She nurtured me with love and care, kindness, selflessness, sacrifice, empathy and many other beautiful attributes, much like the ones her mother had demonstrated to her. My mother's constant and unfailing love helped to balance things out growing up. It helped to preserve my sanity. Unfortunately, change came as a result of things getting worse and that was how I became a ward of the court, placed in the foster care system, and eventually with a relative. Why wasn't my father removed from the home? Why should I have been punished for what he did?

Why was insult added to injury?

At home, every word and action was under scrutiny, so I chose not to speak. I internalized everything and struggled to understand and verbalize my experiences since I was taught to keep my thoughts and feelings quiet because they were not relevant. My struggle felt like hopelessness, helplessness, loneliness, rejection, numbness, and captivity where nothing mattered, nobody cared and I often felt like the walking dead. The anguish and sorrow I felt was never ending. Add to this violence, not consistent, but worse sporadic and unpredictable. There were some precursors, but they were not always reliable. I had a nightmare a few years ago about being huddled with my little sister in the closet. We were anxious and afraid. We heard the loud thud of footsteps coming up the stairs and into our house. That's when I realized, I lived this nightmare. I often would hear my father's footsteps coming up the stairs and into the house and become very anxious. I never knew what was going to happen next. Would he go to sleep or would the terror begin? Usually, it was the latter. The aftermath of his terror was often evident on my mother's face the next day.

I remember an incident that occurred when I was about 11. I enjoyed going to the corner store to play video games whenever I could get my hands on a quarter. I would get so distracted at the store as I watched others play Joust. Well, I guess I must have been distracted too long because when I got home my father was furious. I never could understand what I did to make him so angry. As I walked past him, he punched me in the lower back of my head. All I remember after that was waking up in my bed with my mother and sister at my side. His punishments never seemed to fit the offense.

The drugs and violence in my home took so much away from me. I lost my childhood and the opportunity to grow up with my siblings. Stability and love were taken from me. During the worst of times, such as my being placed in foster care, God took hold of my family and worked on us individually and collectively. We have learned how to love, how to be peacemakers, and how to become better parents, sons and daughters. God is so awesome!

Growing up, my family was so closed I thought everyone lived like I did. I thought everyone's father was like mine. One day as I walked to school, I decided to go to my best friend Bria's house. We usually met at the park, but that day she was late. What I saw when I walked into her home was bittersweet. Bria was sitting on her daddy's lap as he tickled her and then she asked if he could comb her hair. Before she walked out of the house to go to school, she gave him a big kiss and a hug.

Her dad responded, "Have a good day at school Bria. I love you!"

I visited often after that. Even though it hurt to see all of the attention and love Bria was getting from her daddy, I was happy for her. This served as a corrective experience for me. I learned that there were fathers who were kind and gentle. I screamed inside and felt as if I had a boulder on my chest because I had accepted that I may never know this kind of love.

A New Place to Call Home

As a result of my family dynamics, and a joint decision between my mother and the court system, I eventually went to live with my maternal aunt, Titi Yoly. I am so grateful that my aunt was willing to alter her life for me and give me a new place to call home. Life with my aunt was less complicated, in some ways. I faced different challenges: adjusting to a new neighborhood, friends and a whole new set of rules. I struggled with finding my own voice and identity. My identity was ascribed to me by my father. I was what he said I was. Stupid, a slut, a nobody, the cause of all his woes and the list didn't end there. I didn't dare challenge or deviate from the way things were when I lived at home. Now that I had the freedom to exercise my own thoughts and actions, I was consumed with anxiety and worry regarding their validity. As a teenager, I struggled with the person I was and the person I wanted to be. I never took part in the decision making process and now at 14, I was making most of the decisions. No one, other than my mother (and only from time to time for fear of being chastised by my father), ever asked me how I felt or what I thought about certain situations—about any situations. I rarely, if ever verbalized my opinion. Now I had all of the freedom in the world to do it, but my spirit was damaged and broken. It was literally like learning how to talk for the first time.

Fourteen

I was an oxymoron: a pretty ugly girl. I didn't see what others saw in me when I looked in the mirror. My closest friends were goonies and social rejects, which is exactly how I felt inside.

As a matter of fact, my best friend from high school visited me recently and said, "Do you remember how all of the boys liked you?"

My reply was, "No." I felt so upset by her question because the way she recalled things did not coincide with my recollection of things. We both experienced the same situation differently. Was that even possible? Was it the result of the trauma I had experienced as a child? How I saw myself had everything to do with what I had been told and how I had been treated as a child. It had everything to do with a lack of identity formation as a child, teenager and young woman.

I had many new experiences at the age of 14. I had sex for the first time, became a ward of the court and accepted God into my heart.

I recall being asked by the social worker assigned to me by the court system, "Where do you see yourself in a year? Three years? Five?"

I answered, "Pregnant and on welfare."

At the time, I was being facetious. Later, it became a self-fulfilling prophesy. God had a plan for my life and the enemy another. I was oblivious to both. Soon after moving in with my aunt I gave my heart to God. Although I knew God, I didn't understand what it meant to have a relationship with God. I strayed and put the love of a man above my Heavenly Father's love. God never left my side. I gave my heart to Him (although divided) and He worked with it. He never left me and often gave me beautiful signs that I was His and belonged to Him.

At the age of 14, I didn't fully understand sex or how it was done. This may sound ridiculous, but it was true—my mind could not grasp how *the two became one.*

I never had the sex talk with mami but she did say, "When you're ready let me know and I will put you on birth control."

Ready for what? The thought scared me to death! With my little sister's approval, I often consulted with her, I had sex for the first time strictly out of curiosity. It was awful and very painful. I couldn't understand what the big deal was about. I never wanted to do it again. My second encounter was more intimate and less painful. What I didn't know nor understand was that sex outside of marriage does a lot of damage, especially to the psyche of a young person who equates sex with love, much like I did.

Transitions

When I met the father of my children he was very popular with the ladies at the house parties where he'd DJ. I stayed so far away from him when he displayed interest in me because I didn't like a lot of attention and wanted no part of it. This only seemed to fuel his desire. I'm sure he thought, *what, a girl who doesn't want to get with me?* I resisted him at first, but after a couple of months, I gave in. He was easy to talk to and really seemed to care about me, but not more than life in the fast lane, fast money, cars and girls. For the next eight years, he was my everything. I found a new identity in him. He was my reason to live, laugh and hope, but the children and I were not enough in his eyes to put an end to the path he was taking.

I loved being pregnant! The thought of life growing inside of me was overwhelming. Life, giving life. I remember the first little butterflies I felt in my innermost being. How frightened and excited I was at the same time. Being pregnant made me feel important and valued. I received more attention and care than I ever did before. I never set out to get pregnant, despite my comment to the social worker. I just never used protection. After two years of no protection, I became pregnant. My pregnancy didn't seem to be a horrible thing to anyone in my close circle. My mother and aunt were very supportive. Most of my family seemed happy. The support I received made being pregnant at a young age bearable. In school, I was placed in the Young Mother's Program which really provided the academic support I needed to succeed.

Becoming a mother was intimidating. I now had to care for someone other than myself, and I could barely do that. I felt so vulnerable. My baby depended on me for everything and I had nothing to offer but love. Instinctively, I prayed over my daughter Vanessa and two years later, over my son DeeJay before leaving the hospital when they were each born. I dedicated them to God even though I wasn't yet living for Him. I wanted a better life for them, better than mine. My overwhelming love for my children and the influence of my 10th grade social studies teacher, as you'll read later, would be the motivation behind my going to college.

Hope Deferred Makes the Heart Sick

Hope came through my surrender to Jesus Christ, my Savior and Redeemer. At the age of 23, I was at a crossroads. Would I continue to live this life of destruction or surrender my life over to God? I often heard God's voice in my head, especially when I was not living for Him. I knew He was calling me to Him. Right before leaving my children's father, I remember going out to "afterhours" party and feeling sickened by all of the horrible things I witnessed. Afterhours were planned parties every day of the week, usually from 2 a.m.-7 a.m., where any and every thing happened. People of all ages would be doing drugs. Kids were introduced to drugs. Men were having sex with underage girls or worse, tricking them out. Guns were put to people's heads and hit men breezed into town from NYC or Philly just for a night to do a hit. On one occasion, I went and sat outside of the house hosting the afterhours party. It must have been 3 or 4 in the morning when this church van passed by, the gentleman inside quickly backed up to check on me.

The man got out of the van and asked, "Are you okay? Do you need me to take you somewhere?"

I felt so afraid for him, if he only knew the chaos that was going on inside, he wouldn't have stopped.

I quickly said, "I'm okay, thank you."

He hesitated as if he didn't want to leave me there. I recognized God was speaking to that man's heart and mine, letting me know that He cares for me, giving me hope.

I didn't use drugs or partake in the festivities at these parties. In many ways, it served as a reminder of what was taken from me as a child and what could be taken from me now as a parent. I felt so out of place. Still, I frequented the parties because I feared losing my children's father. I knew I had some choices to make and they seemed impossible. I wondered who I was and what I wanted to do with my life? I knew this lifestyle would take more than just my soul, it would take my life, my breath, my children. That thought was unbearable. I had no choice. I struggled for a year before I could muster up enough courage to leave my children's father. My sister, Alicia stood by me unwavering. She also spoke into my life and encouraged me by telling me how beautiful I was and how I deserved better. This made me so angry because she didn't understand the fear I'd have to cross through to get to the other side. She never gave up on me and gave me hope to break free. She's my hero. Had I given in and settled into that lifestyle, this story could have ended very tragically. What waited for me on that road was death. I probably would have become a heroin addict like my father was in the past or ended up in jail or dead. I wanted something more for my little ones. I had to put my hope and trust in God. I realized that the choices I made then would affect the generations to come. DeeJay was 3 years old and Vanessa was 5.

I remember DeeJay saying to me, "I hate you. You made my papi-daddy leave."

Oh how that hurt. He couldn't understand, nor measure the consequences for staying in that relationship, but now at 22 he understands that I was motivated by love to make the best decision for all of us.

Going to church was a big transition for me. I had to change my frame of mind and lifestyle, but I rejoiced at the thought of a new and better life. Michael Peace is one of the pastors who early on spoke into my life.

I remember attending a ministry for young adults and Michael pointing and saying, "Woman of God!"

I looked behind me to see to whom he was speaking, but there was no one behind me. He was speaking to me! I certainly couldn't see it, nor feel it, but he was speaking life into my brokenness, filling me with hope.

As Michael Peace says, "Can anything good come out of the hood? Come and see!"

The road to success began during my 10th grade year in high school, I was pregnant and attending the Young Mother's Program. This is where I met Mrs. Mitchell, my Social Studies teacher. She spoke life over me, nurturing resilience in me by telling me how smart I was and how I should go to college. At the time I couldn't receive her words because I was in such despair. A few years later, her life-changing words came back to me and with the assistance of Sheryl Gonzalez at Rochester Educational Opportunity Center (REOC), I started my college career at Monroe Community College. God was calling me to do great things at a time when I was a single mother on welfare. I couldn't see the path that lay before me. But I needed, and decided, to step out in faith.

With God's help, I went to college, but it wasn't easy. When I started at Monroe Community College at the age of 21, I struggled. I didn't believe in myself and didn't think college was for me. I started thinking *what other options do I have?* The answer was simple: none! I could either stay broke or get serious about school. Early on in college I had to take statistics in the summer when many of my friends were failing this course during a regular semester. On one occasion, while on campus, I shared my desire to take statistics in the summer with my math professor at the time but she insisted that I was not capable of completing this course in the summer. As you can imagine, I was devastated, I needed this course to graduate.

A total stranger who overheard the entire conversation quickly walked up to me and said, "Do not let anyone tell you what you can and cannot do."

I took the course and got a B! This taught me to believe in myself and helped to shape my identity as a smart, courageous, and capable woman.

I went on to SUNY Brockport and struggled with being the only Latina in all of my classes. I was often the topic of discussion and the expert on *mi gente* (my people) and that of African Americans. I recall my classmates asking my grades on papers and my fear of sharing my grades because they might be lower than theirs. The opposite was true, their grades were always lower than mine, and finally, they stopped asking. I graduated from Brockport with the highest honors, summa cum laude and then went on to complete my masters at the University at Buffalo in a year! I am so glad I stepped out in faith 19 years ago!

It's hard to express everything in a chapter, so please don't think my road to success was not full of snares, closed doors and lost opportunities. Occasionally, someone would forget to pick me up from school, so I'd walk home. Sometimes, I wouldn't have money to eat at school, so I'd wait and eat at home. I made many sacrifices and made no excuses. I kept my eyes on the prize. After two years of college, welfare threatened to close my case making it more difficult than it already was to finish college with two little ones.

I said, "Go right ahead, I am going on to do my bachelors!" They never closed my case and I am so proud of myself for not giving into fear. When I got accepted into UB, I had no money and no car! I used my mami's car and commuted, but soon received the Arthur A. Schomburg Fellowship Award for academic excellence and bought myself a car! Don't stop. Keep moving. Ask yourself, how badly do I really want it?

Promotion

After 12 successful and wonderful years as a school social worker, I wanted to move into administration. The problem was our district was in a season of budget cuts. Four years after completing my administrative certification, I was restless and frustrated. One day I just sat, cried and prayed with my husband. I shared how I had no favor in the district and would probably never become an administrator. Little did I know that my supervisor, Audrey Lewis-Cummings, was looking to hire someone for an administrative position. She shared with me how my name popped into her mind and how I kept coming back to mind when she thought of who would be a good candidate. She offered the position to me just a few hours after my husband and I had prayed together. God had already worked everything out in my favor! Thank you Audrey for giving me the opportunity to realize success as an administrator!

Working with homeless youth has been both difficult and rewarding. It is empowering to be able to assist and give homeless youth a voice and hope. It helps to have had my own struggles, some similar to theirs. When they look at me now they cannot tell that I was a troubled youth, stuck in a pit of despair with no end in sight. But that changed when someone spoke life over me and gave me hope.

As the Associate Director of the Homeless Education Program, I understand what the definition of homelessness is under the McKinney-Vento Act. The Act has been in place since 1987, I was 16 years old then and considered a ward of the court and temporarily placed with a relative. In McKinney-Vento terms, I was an unaccompanied youth that was doubled up with a relative. Before this, my mother, sister and I stayed at the Alternative for Battered Women shelter. I must have been 11 or 12, both circumstances qualified me as a McKinney-Vento student, the very same program I now oversee.

Self-Esteem & Identity

Over the years, I have identified and adopted the attributes and characteristics I see and love in others, especially the strong, loving ladies in my life. Despite the pain of my childhood and my many poor choices, I have made it a priority to learn from my mistakes and not make the same mistake twice. First and foremost, I've learned to be true to myself. I have learned to value genuineness, and have developed empathy towards others. I now understand that conflict is not always a bad thing, and in some cases has helped to shape my identity. You would think that after so much suffering and violence I would be a hateful person, but I am not! I love people, even the most vile and ugliest of people. God has guarded and healed my heart from bitterness and unforgiveness.

Most of all I have learned to value me as a Latina, full of life and love for the beautiful culture I was born into. I thank God for the Latinas He used to influence me on my journey: Sheryl Gonzalez, Isabel Hernandez, Luz Delgado-Rhodes and Gladys Burgos-Pedraza. I must share a recent experience with you, one in which I was overwhelmed with pride and joy and brought to tears. Almost a year ago, I, along with my husband who was presenting a paper, attended the Puerto Rican Studies Association (PRSA) Conference at SUNY Albany. I had never seen so many Puerto Ricans that were well educated, many had PhDs. Don't believe the hype! The images in the media are most often negative and leave a misleading impression generalized by the ignorance of the masses. I was enlightened and never felt so proud of being a Latina.

Forgiveness & Restoration

Years later, my father and I reconnected, and today I can say I really love him. At 17, I started going to church again, and this time it was my father that would come and pick me up and take me. He seemed so different; somber and broken. I know he was trying really hard to make up for all of the pain and suffering he had caused me. He often would hug me and tell me he loved me, but back then, I was not ready to receive his affirmations. Every time he touched me I cringed because he had often used his hands to hurt me. After a few years of his persistence, I was able to forgive my father and learn to love him. Despite my prayers asking for him to disappear, he never left us. He later shared that he had never left because he had never met his father. As an adult, I understand my father suffered many things and has his own story to tell. As I look back, I have found happy memories of my father playing with us. During sudden and heavy rain falls, while the sun was still out, my father would often play with us in the rain. My father would always express the need to work hard, whether it be at roller skating or on homework. This value has stayed with me and has developed tenacity in me. One of the happiest and redeeming moments was when my father sang *Butterfly Kisses-* to me as I walked down the aisle at my wedding.

Wife & Mother

My greatest success is being a good mother and wife. When I met my husband, Alexci, I had already graduated from college and was working as a school social worker. My children were 8 and 10. Before meeting Alexci, I felt like I would never be married and would die alone.

Their father often said, "Who's going to want you with two kids?"

He seemed to be right. Men would be very interested in me until they knew of my children and then they'd disappear. Alexci is the only man that stuck by me. He actually thought I had 3 or 4 kids because I always took my friend's kids or neighborhood kids to church with me! My having children, I am sure was scary for him but it wasn't enough to scare him away. As a teen mother and a single mother, I had to cope with the stigma and negative stereotypes associated with these groups.

The first few years of marriage were horrible! I was a lioness, very protective over her cubs and he was an inexperienced bachelor learning how to be an instant husband and father. What a beautiful mess we were. We hung in there and fought a good fight and years later we can truly say that we are blessed with children who love us, as much as they love each other. I now know the love of a man who cares and values my thoughts, feelings and opinions. We're a beautiful family, not perfect, but always growing, forgiving, learning, sharing, loving and laughing.

The Best is Yet to Come!

And so the chapter of becoming a mother as a teen has some closure. I am passionate about the chapters to come. Over the last 19 years, God has given me a free spirit and a love of life. I am less anxious and worried than I have ever been. It could be because I have had to trust God in life and death situations. Pursuing life and all that it entails gives you a new appreciation for life and puts things into perspective.

Thank you God for replacing my brokenness with a crown of beauty and giving me a wholesome recipe for life: live simply—don't over complicate your life by worrying about things that may never come to pass; every day is new and is a gift—what happened yesterday is the past, learn from it and make better choices today; forgiveness is the beginning of healing for you! Good, bad, or ugly, this is my story. Some of my hardest times led to some of my greatest! To God be the Glory!

Author's Corner

Biography: E.C. Reyes is a native of Rochester, New York. Despite struggling through high school and being a young mother, Elizabeth went to college at the age of 21. By the age of 26 she had completed her masters. She attended Monroe Community College and continued her education at the State University of New York at Brockport where she graduated summa cum laude with a bachelor's in social work.. Elizabeth continued to graduate with academic distinction when she went on to the University at Buffalo's Advanced Standing Program, earning a master's in social work. In 2005, Elizabeth completed her post graduate certification in educational administration. She has worked in the Rochester City School District for 15 years, 12 of which she worked providing direct support to students as a school social worker. For the past three years, she has been the Associate Director of the RCSD's Homeless Education Program working with one of the most at-risk and vulnerable populations in the district, homeless students and their families.

Acknowledgments: I wouldn't be where I am today without all of the many sacrifices and exemplars made by the strong, courageous and loving women in my life, both family and friends. My grandmothers, Nereida Pacheco & Georgina Garcia, my mother, Alicia Santana, my aunt, Yolanda Santana, and my one and only biological sister, Alicia Olmeda (I have to differentiate because God has blessed me with so many sisters I love and am so grateful to have in my life!) To my faithful and devoted husband, Alexci Reyes, who was willing to look deeper and has loved harder than any man I've ever known. A very special thank you to my wonderful gifts from God, who have inspired and continue to inspire me to hope and succeed, my children, Vanessa, DeeJay, Adonai and Lexci. To everyone with whom I have shared my dream of writing and has said, "You can do it!" Thank you for believing in me. You know who you are. To LaShunda Leslie-Smith for empowering us and giving us the opportunity to retell our stories, under our terms, with dignity and inspiration thank you!

Contact Info:
Elizabeth Reyes
https://www.facebook.com/lisicreyes
Phone: 585-851-9614

SEVEN

I REFUSE TO BE A STATISTIC
Debbie Martin-Garcia

My name is Deborah Martin-Garcia. I was born in London England in 1971. In this chapter I share with you my personal and emotional journey of how it was for me to be a teenage mother, the whys and the how's and the ups and the downs. I truly hope my story inspires and empowers you to overcome setbacks and struggles in your life and helps you to dream big and believe in yourself.

The Rude Awakening

I woke up sweating and my heart was racing. I was so scared. As I wiped the sweat from my forehead, I remember thinking I am so glad that was only a dream. As I turned around to hug my mum, I felt something move. I froze for a second. There it was again; something was moving inside me. I slowly backed away from my mum and laid on my back, looking at the ceiling. Now my heart was beating faster and harder 'till I could hear my heart beating in my ears. I wasn't dreaming; I must be pregnant.

Was that the baby moving inside me? It must be, did mummy feel the baby move? What if she did? Is she going to beat me? My mind was going all over the place asking questions and answering them at the same time. The conversation I had with the doctor a few months earlier rang in my head.

"Have you had unprotected sex?" he asked.

"What's that?" I replied.

"It's sex without a condom or the pill."

"Oh, we didn't use nothing like that," I said in an unconcerned, naive voice.

"Ok, there is a strong possibility you may be pregnant," he replied. "Take this to the hospital and they will give you a pregnancy test," he said as he wrote on a sheet of official paper.

All I could think was *pregnant! I can't be pregnant. I am only 14, and we only had sex a couple of times.* And by we, I meant me and this handsome older guy that lived round the corner from me. He was kind of my boyfriend, well, that's what I thought. He said he liked me a lot and would pick me up in his car and we would kiss and touch each other. 'Till one day, it went further than that. I didn't really get the chance to think about whether I wanted to do it, it just happened. I only went to the doctor's because my breasts were tender and they hurt, not because I thought I might be pregnant. I thought he was going to give me some cream and send me on my merry way.

As the thought of being pregnant seeped in, I felt sick in my stomach. Light headed, I made my way to the bathroom. I was swamped with a world of emotions: fear, dismay, and bewilderment. I slumped myself onto the toilet seat as tears rolled down my face. I wanted to scream. I started punching my legs as anger swelled inside of me. *How can I be pregnant? I'm so stupid! How can I tell mum this? I am such a disappointment! My life is over! I have messed up my whole life and brought shame to my mum!* These thoughts, and others, swam in my mind.

Isolation

If only someone could have prepared me for what was to follow. I didn't tell my mum; she actually told me. And as peculiar as it sounds, I was so glad she did. You see, I came from a typical Caribbean home where beating and cursing was the normal way to discipline your children. Naturally, I was too fearful to utter the words, "I'm pregnant". My head would have been clean off my shoulders before I could even finish the sentence. When we got beatings, every word was a lick and the onslaught would go on 'till my mum was exhausted or we got away. True to form, I received a barrage of cussing. I felt like I was going to combust as I fought back tears. My throat was burning like fire and my chest was pounding. I felt like wetting myself. I hated when my mum shouted, matter of fact I hated anyone shouting. The only reason I never got a beating was because I was noticeably pregnant. I was about five months pregnant. Three days later my mum took me to the clinic. I walked a few yards behind her, not knowing where I was going. When we entered the clinic, I didn't know why we were there. These weren't our normal doctors. I thought maybe my mum was too ashamed to go to our regular doctors. I tried not to make eye contact with anyone because I feared they would look at me with disgust. I glanced at my mum a few times for reassurance, but she didn't look in my direction or utter a single word to me. Every time I looked at her my heart sunk and felt heavy. Her silence was killing me slowly. A lady called my name and I froze in my seat. My mum got up and walked towards her. I got up reluctantly, feeling like all eyes were on me, and walked across the room to the lady standing in the open door. After the lady examined me, she told my mum to come over. There I was, laying flat on my back behind the screen, my stomach looking huge. Silly me. I was trying to hold my stomach in before my mum came over so it would look smaller. It didn't move an inch. I will never forget the look on my mum's face, shock and dismay. I know she wasn't expecting it to look that big, I had hidden it well.

The lady said, "As you can see, she is too far gone for a termination."

My mum swung her head round quickly and firmly responded, "Oh no. I don't want her to have an abortion. It's her baby let her have it."

But as we walked out the clinic she turned to me and said, "You're going to have that baby and suffer." Spoken in the most hard core Jamaican accent.

My son's dad was not interested in being a father. He was eight years my senior, had a girlfriend as well as many other girls on the side. I was nothing more than a sex object to him and that was a hard pill for me to swallow. He told me he was going to be there for the baby, but told everyone else the child was not his. I prayed morning and night my baby would look like him so I would be vindicated and there would be no question that he was the father. He was deeply ashamed because he should have known better. I was a minor and he took advantage.

My mum did not attend my hospital appointments and rarely spoke to me. I understood she was angry, disgraced and sadden that her 14-year-old daughter was having a baby, but where was her empathy? She too was a teen mum and could identify with the fear, shame and loneliness I was feeling. The rejection from my mum, my son's dad and my friends was overwhelming. I got stares, frowns and sniggers when I would be on the street, bus or at school. There was no place of refuge. I had nowhere to hide and no one to turn to. I felt worthless and scared for my and my son's future. I cried almost daily and felt isolated and sad, but I put on a brave face. The night before my baby was born, I woke up just after 2 am with what seemed to be mild period pains that went on the whole night. I never thought it could be labor pain, that's how young and unprepared I was. Just after 6 am, my water broke. It was like someone popped a water balloon. I knocked quietly on my mum's door trying to wake her gently.

"Mum, my waters have broken," I said softly.

My mum calmly said, "Ok, I will call the ambulance."

Her soft voice was calm and reassuring. For a moment, it took my focus off the pain. That was the kindest I had heard her voice in months. *Maybe she is going to be there for me after all*, I thought.

My baby boy was born two hours later. I made no noise and took no pain killers. I wanted to cause the least amount of fuss, because I had brought this on myself.

Your shame, My Gain!

Courtney Lewis Martin entered into the world on Thursday, May 15, 1986, at 8.20am weighing 6lbs 12oz. As he came out, I breathed a sigh of relief. *I did it, I am a mum now*, I thought. He looked just like his dad which brought a smile to my face. There was no denying it now.

When I held him for the first time, I was overjoyed. Despite the fact I was fourteen, I was a first time mother who wanted her child. We had a connection. I had talked to him all the time and now, he was here. My beautiful baby boy was here. He had a caramel skin tone, hazel eyes and dark brown curly hair, lots of it, too. Finally, someone I can love and who would love me back. I remember whispering to him, "I'm your mummy." I didn't know how hard it was going to be raising my son. All I knew was that I was going to do my best by him. I knew I could be a good mum despite all the negative voices around me telling me *you'll never amount to anything; you'll be on benefit with lots of children from different men.* These negative voices were coming from family, from the people who were supposed to love and help guide me. Instead, they put me down. The more negative things they said to me, the more I wanted to prove them wrong. I would not be a statistic! I made up my mind I was not going to have any more children unless I were married. Mum soon came to accept the fact I had a son and was kind enough to allow us to remain in her home. I was venturing into motherhood with little guidance, but was glad for it. I didn't want anyone to raise my son but me. I knew my mum loved me, but work and studying caused her to neglect things I felt were important. I wanted to be there for my son, more than my mum and dad were there for me.

I had adult responsibilities but was only fourteen. I even breast fed him until he was two years old. I would take him to the park often, partly to go on the swings and slide myself, after all, I was still a child. I remember buying him his first bike and teaching him to ride, we were inseparable. Going to school and being a mum was hard. I would drop Courtney of at nursery in the morning before school and collect him straight after school. Often times, after school my friends wanted me to follow them to the park or to the shops.

They would say, "It won't take long we can go quickly and you can collect Courtney after."

I would explain that I had to go collect my son as he came first. I wasn't asked along very much after that. But, I really didn't care because he was my world. Courtney was my reason for waking up in the mornings and my reason for wanting to do the best I could at school. He made me laugh and smile through all my hard courses and exams. He would wipe away my tears when things got too hard—he loved me unconditionally. Because of him, I wanted to prove that he was not the mistake everyone said he was. Rather, he was the one who gave me the drive and determination to succeed.

A New Me!

My life totally changed in 1991. Courtney was 5 years old and had settled well into full-time school. He was very outgoing and very handsome. He was liked by his peers and teachers. I was at college studying technology. I soon met and married my husband Carlos in 1993. Carlos had Bianca, a daughter from a previous relationship, and I had Courtney. Courtney and Bianca found it hard to adjust to their new lives. They both were used to being the center of their parent's attention. Now they had another sibling and another adult in their lives. Financially, we had little, but we had each other and that seemed to be enough.

We went on to have three boys, Dan'el, Terr'el and Ethan. I was a housewife who spent a lot of time with the children. I was able to see their plays, go on trips, and drop and collect them from school. I wanted more out of life. So in 2001, I started a child care business which enabled me to be there for my children and to make a good income. I loved being around children. They made me laugh and I adored their innocence. The business soon flourished as word of mouth started to spread. My husband quit his job and came to work with me full time. We bought our first home, a new car and we were able to go on family holidays.

From Bad to Worse

Even though things were going well on the surface, I wasn't happy, not completely. Inside, I was sad and empty. In December 1999, we lost a baby boy. I was five and a half months pregnant. I gave birth to him at home less than two hours after coming back from the hospital. I called out to my husband to call an ambulance. Carlos came to the bathroom where I held our lifeless son in my arms.

His eyes instantly filled with tears as he uttered, "Oh, Debbie."

"Can you believe it's a boy?" I said teary-eyed, but smiling.

This would have been my fifth son! We both looked at him, hugged each other and cried. At the hospital, I looked at my son. He was fully formed except for his eyes. He had nails on his little fingers, faint nipples on his chest and gums in his perfectly formed mouth. The doctor said it was just one of those things; there was no logical explanation for it. This was the first time I left the hospital without my baby. I was inconsolable on the drive home. *My baby is there, by himself,* I thought. I wanted him with me. I often cried in secret. I questioned God. I questioned my faith. It was a difficult time for us all. I questioned which would be worse, God taking him now, or when he was five years old when I had gotten to know and love him? I concluded I preferred it this way, this started the process of my healing and coming to terms with my loss.

We spent the next few years going through what seemed to be the hardest, most traumatic time in my life. Our daughter was diagnosed with Hodgkin's Lymphoma in September 2002. I was so angry. As a family, we agreed to get through this. After all, we lost a child and came out fighting. But Bianca was scared just like any 13-year-old would be.

She looked me in the eyes and asked, "Mum, am I going to die?"

I fought back tears as I answered, "No. I believe you have a future and destiny and I don't believe you will die until you fulfill it."

I meant it. Even though I knew nothing about cancer, I prayed continually and left it in God's hands. Every so often, doubt would creep in taunting me, *what about your son, he died?*

"Yes," I would answer, "but, she's a different child with a different destiny."

I found if I didn't stay focused, fear, panic and helplessness would overwhelm me. Bianca at times would cry and refuse her treatment and medication. I would encourage her, insisting it would not be forever and that we'd get through it. She went to school when she was strong enough and seemed to be dealing with it well. I would tell her how proud I was of her. God was faithful and our daughter had the all clear in 2003 after nine months of chemotherapy. In November 2003, our son told me he got a girl pregnant. He cried and tried to explain the situation. I really expected better of him, because Courtney was an 'A' student, very sensible and level headed, and more importantly, he had Christian values. He knew how emotionally hard it was for me being a teenager mother. Now here he was, my 17-year-old son, Courtney, about to embark on the journey to fatherhood.

I wish I could say that was the worst of it. In January, 2004, my 15-year-old daughter told us she was pregnant before she ran away to social services. When it started to sink in, it felt bittersweet. Bitter, because she was so young, and I wanted her to experience life not as I had, having to raise a child when you're a child yourself. Sweet, because the doctors had told us that our daughter would not be able to conceive naturally because the chemotherapy would destroy her eggs. They were wrong. I was fully broken and confused. My heart was heavy and I just felt like I couldn't take any more. The grandsons were born five months apart and I was happy that my daughter and my grandson's mother were ok after having their babies. I took an active role in supporting both mums and spent a lot of time with my grandsons building a bond. Unfortunately, cracks formed in my marriage. There were lots of arguments which lead to fights and, on occasions, police were called. My husband was no longer going to church and I was not being supported at home. His lifestyle changed. He was partying, drinking and smoking. I tried to understand the whys behind his change. Did the events of the last few years overwhelm him too? Was this his way of coping? At times I felt suicidal. Other times, I felt like I was going mad. I couldn't understand why my life was in such turmoil. I was still attending church and praying for a change—that was my only hope. I would listen to empowering words that gave me hope on Sunday, but lived defeated all week. I disliked my husband, my home life and myself. I wanted to hide away until it was all over, but I couldn't. I was going to have to live through this hell.

In the spring of 2005, hell took its toll and I collapsed in the kitchen. My oldest son Courtney found me on the floor. I saw nothing or heard nothing. I came to with Courtney calling me and trying to help me to my feet. I soon realized there was something seriously wrong. My body felt heavy and I was slurring so badly my son could not understand me. At the hospital, they said it seemed like a mild stroke, but could not see anything on the CAT scan. When they sent me home, I took time off from work to recover and my speech returned after a couple of weeks. Unfortunately, my health took a turn for the worse. I now had a heart murmur along with gynecological and kidney problems. The doctors believed my deteriorating health stemmed from the stress of losing our baby, our daughter getting cancer, my children becoming teenage parents and my marriage failing. For me, there was no light at the end of the tunnel, at least that's how I felt. My church friends were prayerful and loving and gave wise counsel. I spoke to Claudine, my best friend, daily. She was always supportive and encouraging. It was really hard for friends and family to relate because they had not been where I was and didn't really know a way forward for me except through prayer and keeping positive.

They tried to help, but what I needed was beyond their capacity to handle; it was going to take more.

Remember, Release and Refocus

This was bigger than all of us. As I started to spend more time by myself, I read self-help books and books on how to overcome stress. I needed to help myself. Nobody knew me better than I knew myself except God. I knew my life was in turmoil, but I didn't want it to impact my health the way it was any longer.

My bishop, Wayne Malcolm, said one Sunday morning, "You can't change the weather but you can change your clothes."

That was life changing for me. I started to look at my life and asses where I was. I began looking at the past. I always used to think, and say that I had had a good childhood. But the more I thought about my past, the more I remembered things I had blocked out. How did being sexually abused from the age of 8 years old slip by me without a second thought? Or, my dad not being around much because he had another family? Or, my mum not being around because of work and being left out on the streets in the rain looking for my brothers? And what about my being physically and emotionally abused? My childhood was anything but good. Looking back helped me put things into perspective. The fact that my dad wasn't about made me long for that father figure, acceptance and wanting to be loved by a man. Being sexually abused by people I knew that weren't much older than me, but old enough to know better, gave me an appetite for sex at a young age. Being sent to foster care made me feel rejected and unloved. Being beaten and told I was stupid and ugly by foster parents stripped me of confidence and kept my self-esteem low. Being left alone for hours, because my single mother had to work to make ends meet, made me easy prey for anyone looking to take advantage. You see, the journey leading up to and then being a teenage mother had all the right ingredients for a breakdown like this. Knowing this made me angry and hurt even more; but it was necessary for me to face in order for me to move forward. I had held it in and now it was time to let it all go before I ended up crazy, or worse, killing myself.

I was on a quest for a new me. The process would be long and hard but worth it in the end. As my mindset changed, so did my image. I lost weight and I gained a voice. I began sharing my experiences with others to give them hope and strength. I have since become a Nero Linguistic Programming practitioner, counselor and life coach. I was given the opportunity to be the key note speaker at Dare 2 Dream, one of United Kingdom's dynamic conferences for women hosted by my dear friend, Mrs. Karen Allen, who always listened and believed in me. I studied to be a supervisor/manager with the desire to start my own nursery school one day. I was doing things I've always wanted too but never thought I could. As I embarked on a very long healing process, I started to gain confidence. I believed in myself. My faith blossomed and I forgave those in my past which released me to move forward.

Today, I speak life, health and strength into my life and all those I come into contact with. When my best friend Claudine was diagnosed with breast cancer in 2010, I was able to provide care and support. I encouraged her to think positively. I was becoming the amazing beautiful woman God had created me to be. Even my mother noticed, which was hard to accept at first, but not anymore. It's been a long process to get to where I am today. Despite the end of my marriage and dealing with my youngest son, Ethan's, cancer diagnosis, I am a more content and positive person who has a brighter outlook on life.

My son Courtney is now 27, with his own children. He tells me often how much he loves me and how proud he is to call me his mum.

I tell him, "I love you too, son. You're amazing! You make me proud."

In the end, I didn't become that statistic people said I would. Remember, life happens. What really matters is how you deal with it. Finally, I have embraced my past and I am focused on my future.

Author's Corner

Biography: Deborah Martin-Garcia is a mother of four amazing sons and one daughter. She takes pride and joy in her two angelic granddaughters and three energetic grandsons. Deborah successfully founded her own childcare business in 2001. Along with this she runs a family business called Deb-On-Air Events and Balloon Services. She has a diploma in counseling, and in Nero Linguistic Programming, NLP and is also a Life Coach. Deborah was the keynote speaker at one of United Kingdom's Dynamic Women Conferences Dare 2 Dream in 2010, where she empowered and motivated the women to overcome life's struggles. Deborah continues to empower and motivate whomever she comes in contact with, including her children and grandchildren, who through her mentoring are doing her proud.

Acknowledgments: To God, my best friend, without you this project would not be possible. Thank you for not giving up on me. To Carlos, thank you for giving me our 5 amazing children. To my champions, Courtney, Dan'el, Terr'el, and Ethan, you make me proud to be your mum. I love you all so much; this is for you. You all give me strength to carry on when I feel like quitting. To Bianca, I hope this book inspires you to be the best you can be. To my grandchildren, Juel, Shakiah, Harley, Saisha and Myson, you guys make me so happy; you are so much fun to be around. Mum, you have been my friend as well as a mother. Thank you. I love you more than words can say. To Paul, my big bro, you are like my twin, you totally understand me. Thanks for all your love and support. To my dad and my brother, Micheal, I hope this makes you both proud. To my Bishop, Wayne Malcolm, this has been a long time coming- thank you for being my spiritual father. To my best friend, Claudine, my sister from another mister who has been there through the laughter and the tears, thank you from the bottom of my heart. To Karen, thank you for believing in me and connecting me with LaShunda. To Garry W., thank you for listening and helping me to move forward to the next chapter in my life. To Jennifer Matthews and Jacqui John, you will forever be in my heart. And to all my friends and family that have prayed and gone through the hard times and good times with me, I truly love and appreciate you all. To my new friends, LaShunda, Maisha, Tiffiney, LaToya, Tanishia, Charlyn, Sarah-Elizabeth, Elizabeth, Stephanie, Rosa, Shenita, and Shiera, you are all amazing women with a great story to tell, it's been an honor doing this collaborating with you all. May God continue to bless you as you bless others.

Contact Info:
Debbie Martin-Garcia
www.debbiemartingarcia.co.uk
debbiemartingarcia@gmail.com
Facebook: https://www.facebook.com/dmartingarcia1
Phone: 7929850944

EIGHT

THE EVOLUTION OF ME
Maisha Beard

Basketball and Boyfriends

High school basketball announcer voice:

The basketball is being dribbled by point-guard Zee Mullen and she's looking on the inside for center Maisha Beard, who stands 6ft tall as a junior! Rica flanks Maisha as a power forward and Mel rotates between the shooting guard and small forward positions. This team has the potential to dominate this year's section 5 tournament! Zee fakes for the three-pointer, passes the ball deep into Beard, and she makes the lay up! These girls are unstoppable! Zee drops 5 three-pointers and Beard pulls down a record nineteen rebounds!

We won that game against East High and I was finally a basketball star! It was the first game of the 1989-90 school year and the following day, I was reading about myself and Zee in a newspaper article! As the basketball season progressed, I began to realize that my name was buzzing around the city of Rochester, especially in the girls' basketball coaches' circles. Phone messages from various college coaches began to fill up

111

my father's answering machine, and there was no doubt that I would go to a Division 1 college and play basketball. Perhaps I would make the Olympic Team!

My parents lived vicariously through me and I enjoyed every moment of it! My grades put me on the high honor roll. My boyfriend, Michael, was on the boys basketball team and he and I spent every spare moment together. Unbeknownst to my father, I would sneak out of the house at 5am and head over to Michael's house before school. We were both 17 years old and we were in love. We both manipulated our parents' work schedules to work in our favor. Michael and I were intimate almost every day, often-times twice a day. We always made time for sex. Whether it was at his house, or my own, we would fulfill our sexual desires in his bedroom, the attic, the bathroom, the basement, the outdoors, the indoors, or anywhere we could! It was as if we were nymphomaniacs! The only place that we didn't have sex was in school!

In retrospect, I realized that my risky sexual behavior at an early age was in direct correlation with the fact that I was sexually molested at 5 years of age. According to a 1998 study by the University of Southern California, research showed that girls who were sexually abused as children were far more prone to risky sexual behavior and pregnancy by adolescence. [ii]

This poem is liberating. When I wrote it, I wept for the five year old little girl inside of me. Through my poetry, she is now free.

When She Was Five

Her daughter turned 5 today
Beautiful high spirited little soul without a care in the world
Her virtue and essence is pure
Untainted by the evils and darkness of the world
World winds of cartwheels and cheers and dolls and pig tails with bows
and...
STOP
HER DAUGHTER TURNED 5 TODAY
Like when she was five when he planted an evil seed inside of her
When
Her baby-sitters nephew asked to take her to the store
The babysitter nonchalantly said sure
But the store was never a destination
It was a garage
And with grave anticipation
He stole what was hers
And upon their return
He gave instructions that frightened her
She went to the ladies room and frantically cried as she tried to clean
his STUFF off from her
STUFF not understanding what the STUFF was
She blacked out and suppressed this STUFF until now
Her daughter turned 5
And at 32 years old, the victim became the predator
In search of her prey to retain what belonged to her...
She tried to go to Brother Minister because he was his uncle and
perhaps he can be a mediator
But Brother Minister fumbled the ball and again she's enraged because
her daughter is
5 and her 5 year old self deserves retribution for what was done to her
Who will stand for her!
Investigations led her to the places where he rested his evil head
Headed to his home
She got her husband on the phone and told him her whereabouts and
how if he loved her, he would help her commit murder
Suddenly her voice stopped
Thoughts of her children without a mother was unheard of
She wept

Because MY daughter turned 5
Like I was five in 1979 when he stole what was mine and planted an
evil seed inside of me
I am not defined by what happened to me
I've found healing
In 1977, no one helped me
In 2013, I've claimed the victory
Maisha B. Poetry n' Love ©2013

Michael was the love of my life. My entire existence revolved around him. It was easy to visit Michael because he lived on the next street over from my father and me. Every other weekend, I would try to avoid visiting my mother. Of course, it never worked. A weekend with Mommy meant a weekend away from Michael. It was pure torture! Upon my return home from Mommy's, Michael's house would be the first place that I'd visit. Michael and I would proceed straight to the bedroom to have sex! I'm appalled at myself at this present moment. How dare I have sex in his parent's house while they were home. Or in my grandparent's basement while they were home? Were we serious? I'd say absolutely insane! Yet, my 17-year-old self had no regrets.

Spring Fever: The Struggle

Michael had just gotten back in town from a family trip to Mississippi. I painstakingly waited and anticipated his call. Finally, the phone rang.

"But BOOM DOE!" Michael always made up new phrases that meant absolutely nothing, other than the definition he gave them.

"Hi, Bae!" I exclaimed, in my 17 year-old sexy voice.

We conversed via telephone until he told me that he was on the lower level of the projects that we lived in called Gateway. Families with low incomes, welfare recipients, poor working class people, drug dealers, crack heads, illegal aliens, roaches and mice all took residence in Gateway. The stairs to our townhome smelled of old urine and was embellished with cigarette butts, drug paraphernalia, and on a good day, you might just share the stairwell with a big, fat, juicy rat! Nevertheless, we made the townhome our home. Daddy was a hard working recovering drug addict/alcoholic/domestic violent offender, who was raising his three children.

I immediately hung up the phone and put on my Michael Jordan sneakers that matched my tight fitting red sweat suit and ran down the stairwell to greet him with a huge sloppy kiss! His breath smelled like halls cough drops and his lips tasted like the menthol chap stick that he frequently used. Surprisingly, the odor from the stairwell had no effect on me. I was in the arms of my boyfriend, and Daddy was at his girlfriend's house with my siblings. I had the house to myself.

Michael and I finally left the stairwell and entered the door marked 1499. As the door closed, we began to kiss and feel up each other's bodies like animals in heat. A trail of passion marks on Michael's neck, made it evident that Michael and I were trying to suck the blood out of each other. Michael visited me on the weekends that I wasn't with Mommy and during the times when Daddy and my baby brother and sister were not home. Sometimes, I was so afraid of Daddy's wrath, that I'd make Michael leave. Unbeknownst to me, Daddy would have made plans to sleep at his girlfriend's house and I would be disappointed when Daddy never arrived home, thinking, *Gosh, Michael could have stayed!* On April 14, 1990, one day before Easter Sunday, I assured myself that Daddy would not be returning home that evening due to the aforementioned patterns of staying with his girlfriend overnight. I was wrong. I convinced Michael to follow me upstairs to my bedroom so that we could have sex. We ripped each other's clothes off and devoured each other sexually, in typical 17-year-old fashion. Between the animated moaning and groaning, I noticed that a light was shining through the cracks of my bedroom door.

I whispered, "Michael, was that light on?"

He looked and anxiously answered, "No."

For a moment, we laid there flabbergasted and thunderstruck.

We jumped up and put our clothes on while Daddy called to me angrily, "Maisha, come into my room please."

"I'm coming Daddy."

Tears began to fall from my eyes landing on my red sweat suit, creating perfectly round discolored spots. I wiped my tears with my sweatshirt, left Michael in my bedroom and slowly walked into Daddy's room.

"Yes, Daddy?"

Tears began to fall from my eyes and before I could apologize to my father, his girlfriend's high pitched alto-like voice screamed upstairs.

"James! Is everything ok up there? Something just fell from Maisha's window…and…I think…it's…Michael. He's gotten up! He's staggering! James! James!"

"I was going to let him walk out of my house with dignity!

This boy is going to kill himself!" Daddy exclaimed.

We cleared both flights of stairs in the apartment, and ran down the stairwell and onto the first floor where Michael staggered, in hopes of making it to his aunt's house.

"Bae! Bae! Why did you jump four stories! You could have died!"

I wept uncontrollable as Daddy lifted Michael from the ground and helped him into the car.

"Come on young man! You didn't have to do that man! Now I have to call your parent's and tell them you jumped out of my window, man!"

Michael was silent and clearly out of sorts.

Mr. and Mrs. Johnson walked into the emergency department. I hung my head in shame.

One month later, I began to feel extremely tired and lethargic. Representatives from colleges were flooding Daddy's answering machine inquiring about my choices for college. The scout from Shaw University displayed interest in having me visit their campus. He wanted to recruit me for their women's basketball team. A university in the state of Texas also showed interest in my athleticism. I was excited beyond belief!

After a month passed, I decided Shaw University would be my number one choice for college. I had taken my PSAT's and my Grade Point Average was 3.43. It appeared as though my academic and athletic abilities were a good fit for Shaw. All that was required of me was to have a phenomenal senior year on the basketball court, as well as to obtain my diploma. My parents were gleaming with pride! I was still on punishment after that window fiasco with Michael, nevertheless, life was fantastic, or so I thought. *Why am I so tired? Why am I sleeping so much? These smells are making me sick. I wish that Mel would stop wearing that Bijan oil. It used to smell so good, but now, I cannot stomach the smell.*

A few days later, Mel and I drove to Genesee Valley Park to senior skip day. Mel and I were very close and she displayed a maturity that surpassed her age. Mel was one of my three best friends and I often poured my heart out to her. She had given me my nickname "Mo" and it was an endearing name, one only my dearest friends called me. She was the first person who knew that I was pregnant. I trusted her to keep my secret safe.

The sun kissed her bi-racial complexion as we rode into the park. Mel was as close to perfect as possible. I'm certain that she was the only student who received parental consent to attend senior skip day. Of course, this event was unauthorized and, unbeknownst to us, parents were called and to my surprise, my father rolled up like the cops.

"Yo *Mo!*" said Keith

"Yoooooo, ya crib rolled up on us askin' if we saw you!"

"Yo, ya crib? Yo, he was VEXED!"

There were so many voices coming at me all at once, nevertheless, Keith's voice was the prominent one as he yelled, *"Oh, snap! Yo! Ya crib is pullin' up now!*

"Mel, pull off now!"

Mel pulled off before I could get the door closed! Her mother's 1989 Chevy Lumina was our getaway vehicle. We were all silent. All Mel could think of was getting into trouble if Daddy saw us pull off so recklessly in her Mom's car.

Rica kept saying, "Oh my God, Oh my God, Oh my God!"

"Whew! Mel, you drove this car like a true gangster!" Mel,

Rica and I, were able to laugh after the initial shock.

"Well, I'm already in trouble, so I may as well tell Daddy that I'm pregnant today."

"Yea girl, you may as well," said Mel. Mel was always the voice of reason in our crew. Zee was popular and cool. Rica was pretty and extremely goofy. I was sensitive and sneaky.

Several hours later, my heart pounded in my chest as Mel turned her car into Gateway. We looked at each other. I simply got out of the car as I tried to mentally prepare to tell Daddy that I was pregnant.

As I slowly walked up the steps, I began to have flashbacks to the spring of 1987. I signed papers. These papers contained words and phrases that I did not comprehend. I simply did what my parents told me to do. I was fifteen years young. I was pregnant with Michael's child. Michael was also fifteen years young. My parent's made the decision to terminate the pregnancy. I had no voice, nor did I have rights. When I lay back on the cold hospital table, the doctor asked me if I wanted to follow through with the procedure. Tears fell from my eyes as my feet dangled inside the pulleys and my legs were spread as wide as they could go. I never answered the doctor. Mommy did.

"Yes she does" said Mommy.

Endearingly, she lay on top of me as the loud machine sucked life out of me. My eyes stung as tears snaked from my eyes finding solitude in my ear canal. I felt traumatized and violated. Although my parent's felt as though they were doing what was in my best interest, I resented them for it. I was prepared to run away if they tried to make me do it again, especially after the local pro-life organization gave a presentation in health class. They showed pictures of ten week old terminated embryos. Pictures of tiny feet were held in between two adult fingers. I almost fainted as I ran out of class and vomited. I grew angrier at my parents for what they had made me endure. They stole my heartbeat.

Stolen

They sucked the life out of me
Age 15
There was a heartbeat
Behind the belt of my jeans
A heartbeat
The beat of the heart
Heard at 10 weeks
It was then
The appointment
Like the green mile
I walked it
Painstakingly
It was long
White walls
Like the twilight zone
No color
Just black and white
I touched my belly
I said goodbye
To the heartbeat
Inside of me
Beating so rapidly
Tiny hands
Tiny feet
A human being
Spoke of as an embryo
Yet
A brain has formed
Stolen

Not to be born
It was thievery
Unbeknownst to me
I could have refused
Yet
I didn't have a clue
My parents told me
And so
They sucked the life out of me
At age 15
They stole what belonged to me
Behind the belt of my jeans
I was only 15
Maisha B. Poetry n love ©2013

Fury and resentment from that experience two years prior, gave me the strength to confront my father. I turned my key and slowly walked inside. The smell of incense assaulted my nostrils and I saw Daddy's silhouette on the couch, legs crossed, pointer finger resting on his temple. His eyes were closed, yet, he was not asleep. He was upset about the phone call he received about senior skip day.

"Dad, I'm pregnant, I don't care what you and Mommy say, I'm not having an abortion."

I stood there bold and cold. Daddy looked at me and didn't say one word. I felt as though I had nothing to lose. So, I stood there as if to challenge my father.

Armageddon

It felt as if Armageddon paid me a visit and ended my world. Between the morning sickness and vomiting, along with my father's disgust and disappointment, I became depressed. Almost everyone I loved tried to convince me to abort the pregnancy.

My scholarship to Shaw University would not become a reality if I carried my pregnancy to term. My friends were graduating and heading for college leaving me abandoned and lonely. The thought of being in an abortion clinic again, frightened me physically and emotionally. Mommy wasn't as disgusted as Daddy, nevertheless, she wasn't very pleased.

Mel, Zee, and Rica left for college in August of 1990, which left me friendless and isolated. Rica received a scholarship for Shaw University and I wished that I were by her side.

I had no idea how I would take care of a baby while in high school. My father told me that I had to leave his house. He stated that I needed to figure out a way to care for myself and my unborn child. I cried profusely. My baby sister came in my room and sat on my bed trying to figure out what was wrong with me. I had nowhere to go. My father had abandoned me emotionally and financially. In retrospect, I believe that his decision may have been an attempt to get me to re-evaluate my decision. I didn't. God gave me a second chance—He gave me back the child that I terminated—and I desperately wanted someone to love me unconditionally.

Senior year was no picnic. I was five months pregnant and rumors still circulated about Michael 's attempt to "fly like a super-hero." I lost my position as president of the student government, I was no longer a basketball star, and my teachers were not empathetic to my condition. I felt like a cancerous cell—no one wanted me around. Counselors attempted to place me at an alternative school for young mothers. I declined. I didn't want to be labeled and placed with a group of girls who weren't respected as real high school students among their peers.

Third Trimester

Mommy and I walked to the car after leaving the doctor's office. The air was crisp and cold. It was a typical winter day in Rochester, New York.

"Mommy, tomorrow is my due date and today is Michael's birthday! I hope I have the baby today, January 4, 1991 !"

"That would be nice."

Mommy smiled and we drove back home to Daddy's house.

"Call me if anything happens."

"I will Ma. Bye."

I walked into the townhome and began to look at the baby crib that I had purchased. Unbeknownst to Daddy, I had applied for Social Services and had begun receiving public assistance. My apartment would be ready next month and his wish would be granted.

I'm leaving this house and I'm going to take care of myself, my child, and graduate from high school simultaneously.

"Maisha, come here please."

"Yes, Dad?"

"Baby, I just want to let you know that I'm proud of you and you don't have to leave this house. You and my grandchild can stay here as long as you want."

My heart thundered in my chest. Daddy was sad and I couldn't handle it.

"Daddy, I'm sorry, but I'm leaving next month."

Daddy was speechless. He walked upstairs and closed his bedroom door. Music began to play and I knew that he was saddened.

Transition: Hope

Deuce was a cute, little, chubby wubby baby with a huge smile and curly hair. Michael gave the baby his nickname "Deuce". Deuce's given name was Michael Johnson, Jr. Deuce signified the "second one" in an urban slang sort of way. This was another one of Michael's word choices to which he had given his own definition.

Michael pursued his football career at a state university less than thirty minutes away. I enrolled in a cosmetology school and relied on public assistance grants to sustain Deuce and me.

One-hundred and forty three dollars in food stamps per month and fifty-eight dollars per month for a bus pass for transportation to the Education Opportunity Center for cosmetology classes. I never spent the money on a bus pass. I couldn't afford too. I used it for toiletries and whatnots for Deuce. My white nursing shoes were required for the cosmetology program and wore quickly due to the snow and sleet that I walked in during the winter months. I couldn't afford a pair of boots, nor did I have a hat or gloves. I walked to class with my hands in my pockets and by the time I entered the building, my socks and shoes were soaked. Suddenly, being a teenage mother with no transportation, living off of public assistance, was not as cute as I thought it would be.

Two-Thousand and Nine: Success

"Michael Johnson, Jr.!" announced the principal of Edison Technical and Occupation Education Center.

"Michael!!!! Deuce!!!! M-Jay!!! Let's go!"

Yes! My baby that I'd given birth to while I was in high

school had graduated from high school!

"We did it Michael! We did it! We made it!"

Both Michael and I were in tears by our son's milestone moment. I thought of every person who tried to convince me to terminate my pregnancy with Deuce. I began to reminisce upon my struggle as a teenage mother. I looked at all four of my children and realized that I am blessed beyond measure. After twenty years as a successful and well known cosmetologist, I decided to enroll in Monroe Community College at age 37. My first semester was astounding! I earned myself a grade point average of 3.67! I hadn't written an essay, nor taken any tests of any kind since high school! It was at that moment that I realized that I am smart! I can really do this!

Unfortunately, Michael and I, who had married in 1998, divorced in 2010 and now we live separate lives while co-parenting our children. I continued to pursue my associate's degree and I'm proud to say that I completed my goal! In December of 2012, I earned my associate's in liberal arts and health sciences. In the fall of 2013, I enrolled at the State University of New York at Brockport as a social work major. I have also begun to write and perform poetry, as well as continuing my career as a cosmetologist.

My life has had its share of struggle, hope and triumph. At this very moment, I am successful because I've kicked down barriers and have accomplished what statistics say rarely happens. My children and I are champions and we strive to manifest our highest good through affirming our gifts, transmitting love and believing that we can do and be whatever it is that we desire. We recognize that life is for the living and the pain and anguish of transition can give birth to victory and unprecedented success in all of our endeavors.

The Evolution of Maisha

It *was when she recognized her own splendor, then the world told her she was beautiful*- Meredith Rose⬜

A black butterfly was she
She nested within a cocoon for many years
Safe within the confines of her thoughts
Admiring those who displayed a beauty and strength she dreamed
of
Soft and fragile
Easily broken
Like tissue when wet
Lived life in fear
Fearfully taking baby steps to fit in
Anxiety filled
Pain driven
Merely looking for a place to call a safe haven
Many saw her disparity
Gifted ones saw her potentiality
Her personality remained hidden
Afraid to mention
Anything that would fertilize and grow her strength
Black Butterfly
She cocooned
Shedding the old skin for the new
Shaking trepidation and uncertainties
Replacing it with confidence and maturity
Maturation at its finest degree
Flying effortlessly
The black butterfly is you and you and you and you...
The Black Butterfly is me...
Maisha B. Poetry n' Love ©2013

May the authenticity and transparency of my story bless, encourage, and inspire you. You are a star, and just like the stars that dance across the midnight sky, there is room for all of you to shine.

i A more in depth look at this study can be found at: http://news.usc.edu/sexual-Abuse-Teen-Pregnancy/

Author's Corner:

Biography: Maisha Beard is a licensed cosmetologist and a graduate of Monroe Community College. She attained her AAS in liberal arts at age forty and is now a student at SUNY Brockport majoring in social work. Maisha is a renowned hairstylist and a well-respected spoken word poet in her hometown of Rochester, New York. Maisha is a member of Psi Theta Kappa Honor Society and was inducted in 2010 for her high achievements in her field of studies. Maisha's passion is the uplifting of women through her hairstyling and poetry. Poetically, she has risen and become a well sought after poet and shares her "Poetry n' Love", also her stage name, amongst her community. She is now in the process of completing a spoken word CD/documentary. Maisha has also traveled to Atlanta, California and New York City where she was the assistant hairstylist for well-known celebrities including songstresses, Ciara and Kelis. Her goal is the completion of her bachelor's degree and the attainment of a master's degree to become a licensed master social worker which is a goal that she is destined to reach. Maisha has also been chosen as a panelist on the Women's Foundation of Genesee Valley Voices of Experience Forum for the Empowerment of Adolescent Girls. She prides herself by empowering her four children: Michael Jr., Tyreik, Na'Imah and Maya, and by fueling them with guidance for becoming their best selves. "It was when she recognized her own splendor, then the world told her she was beautiful." Meredith Rose

Acknowledgments: First and foremost, I must thank the Divine Spirit and presence of Creator for my entire existence. I am overflowing with gratitude for LaShunda Leslie-Smith, whose vision has rewarded me the opportunity to share my heart and soul with the world. My beloved Grandparents who have transitioned from this life, Carrie K. Beard and Robert O. Moore, Sr.. May their souls continue to transcend with ease, for I would not exist without their love. To my paternal Grandfather, Willie F. Beard, you are the strongest man on the planet! To my first love, my father, James Beard, Ph.D., you have poured your entire spirit into me. Thank you for raising me and believing in all that I am! Mommy, Cheryl D. Moore, may this make you proud! You're the strongest woman I know and my strength comes from you! To all of my aunts and uncles, only God himself knows how much I love all of you! To Tokeya C. Graham, thank you for inspiring me to keep writing! Your guidance and sisterhood is inspiring! Thank you for believing in me! You're the best professor I've ever experienced! My baby sister and brother, Afi and Nashid Beard, I'm proud that I am your sister and I wouldn't change a thing! Afi, thank you for looking up to me and I pray that I'm as great of a sister to you as you are to me! Nashid, I love you beyond the stars within the sky! To the sister of my soul, Ms. Regina Robinson Doyle, you are my best everything! There aren't enough words within the English language that can define our connection! To Carlisa McCullough, thank you for carrying me when I couldn't carry myself! To my high school sisters in spirit: Melanie McElroye, Zenette Mullen, and Erika Allen, you were there from the beginning and we will always share a special bond. L.Y.L.A.S forever! To Michael Johnson, Sr., we produced amazing children together and after 20 plus years, you still own a special piece of my heart. To each reader, I thank you for allowing my story to touch your heart and fuel your spirit. Finally, yet importantly, I'm thankful to my children: Michael Jr., Tyreik, Na'Imah, and Maya Johnson. I am complete because of you and everything that I do is for you!

Contact Info:
Maisha Beard
www.exclusivelymaisha.com
exclusivelymaisha@yahoo.com
Facebook: https://www.facebook.com/maisha.beard
Twitter: @Poetrynlove
Phone:585-713-4380

LaShunda with Branden age 2

LaShunda with Branden age 18

Charlyn, husband Todd, and
Todd Jr. age 2 months old

Charlyn, husband Todd, Todd
Jr. age 5 and Tahjmere age 3

Elizabeth with her Mother Alicia

Stephanie with Semiyah age 3

Maisha at her baby shower

Maisha with Michael Jr. age 20

Angela with Jayson age 4

Angela with Mookie at age 18

Sarah-Elizabeth with Noah
age 3 months

Debbie with Courtney age 26

Tanishia with Rafael age 3

Tanishia with Rafael age 18

Rosa with NaKisha age 3 months

Rosa with NaKisha age 7

Tiffiney at her High School graduation

LaToya with Teja age 9 months   LaToya with Teja age 17

Shenita with Anthony Jr. at   Shenita with Anthony Jr. age 15
1 week old

Shiera with Christopher age 1 month

NINE

MY BUTTERFLY JOURNEY
Charlyn Elliott

I call this my butterfly journey because a butterfly is a very beautiful creature, but in order to reveal its outer beauty, there is a transformation that must take place on the inside. Just like the butterfly, I, too, had to go through a metamorphosis in my life in order to get to the place where I am today.

My mother was never around and my grandmother raised me. But, even though my grandmother was there, I still longed for a genuine mother-daughter relationship. This is my story; the journey that led to me becoming a teenage mother. Words to describe my journey would include, death, favoritism, runaway, stalked, assaulted, young mother and woman of God. They take me back to April of 1989. This date has more of an effect on me than anyone could ever imagine. Let's start at the beginning.

My Egg Stage

One day, I remember coming home from school only to find out that my mother was sick in a Florida hospital and we had to leave to visit her. By we, I mean my grandmother, my sister and my cousin. You see, I used to live in Florida with my mom but she had gotten herself into some trouble. So much so that she had appeared in an article in the 1978 edition of Jet Magazine, titled *Tough Breaks* and a tough break it was. It left her incarcerated and unable to care for me which ultimately led me to Rochester, New York to be raised by my grandmother. Already having two of my siblings and a host of cousins in her care, she was hesitant to take me. I'm not sure if sharing that with me was a good or a bad thing for me to know, but she did eventually decide to take me in and raise me with my siblings. When we arrived in Florida, we were absolutely spoiled by my great uncle; he had given me my first boom box, which I felt was kind of special. We also went to Disney World and had many other excursions to keep us occupied during my mom's hospitalization. The time came for me to visit my mom in the hospital. Once we got past the red tape, which was my being too young to be in the ICU, I saw my mother, my twin, laying on what was to become her deathbed. She hugged me and said she missed me and she'd come visit as soon as she got better. Soon after the visit it was time to leave Florida. When we arrived back in Rochester; we got a phone call. My mother had died. Even though I didn't have a relationship with my mom, at 11 years old, it was still a hard pill to swallow.

Our flight back to Florida to say our final goodbyes proved to be a journey that opened Pandora's box. I don't know what was worse, finding out that I wasn't my mom's youngest daughter or discovering Ms. Cunningham, my mother, was actually Mrs. Rudolph! I had had no idea she was married. I was told I had a baby sister whom I'd meet for the first time as she said hello and goodbye to a mother she'd never met.

I had never been to a funeral, so I had no idea what to expect. I could not stop crying, seeing her lying there lifeless, realizing how permanent this was, and understanding I would never see this woman who birthed me, ever again.

After some time passed, I asked my grandmother if I could try to find out who my father was and locate his family. Her response to that question changed me. She pretty much told me, she would not try to find my father; she was the one raising me and she was the one that was caring for me. Her tone said it all. I felt as if I had asked the unthinkable. I would never ask anything like that again.

It was hard to hear that from my grandmother. I was the only one she cared for who had never met her father. My sisters and my cousins, they all had other siblings, aunts and cousins on their fathers' side of their families, but I knew nothing of mine. I met all of their fathers, even knew their siblings. I was the only one left wondering to whom I belonged. Don't get me wrong, I knew my father's name; it was on my birth certificate. But at 11, there's only so much I could've done. And by the time I was old enough to find him on my own, it was too late, he had already passed away.

My Caterpillar Stage

Entering my teenage years as a 13-year-old ninth grader, I experienced public school for the first time. I had attended a Catholic school for much of my life. It took some convincing but my grandmother finally registered me at Benjamin Franklin

High School a day before school started. My first day of school put me at ease after seeing nearly half of the people I went to elementary school with, along with others I grew up with. There were so many new things to experience at this school. I wanted to run track. Although short, I thought about playing basketball or even cheerleading, but most of all, I wanted to dance. I just knew I was going to be the next background dancer for MC Hammer. All of those interests where quickly shot down once my grandmother told me I had to go to school and come straight home. Not only did I have to come straight home, but it seemed like she had a tracker on me that went off every time I walked in the house. Like clockwork, I unlocked the door, walked in and the phone rang; she wanted to make sure I was home. I'm sure she meant well, but it left me unable to be a teen. I felt isolated and idle. The constant monitoring and random check-in's forced my hand. I began skipping class, and eventual skipping school all together. This newfound freedom was intoxicating and led to me eventually running away at the age of 14. I ended up camping out in a drug house with my friend and her boyfriend. That life experience was tough to see. The home we lived in had young children. It was heart wrenching to watch these women spend their last bits of money on drugs instead of food for their children. But it still wasn't enough to make me want to go home. What convinced me was meeting this one dealer selling out of the house. He was older and scary. He took an interest in me even though I didn't return his interest. His less than flattering, vain and borderline creepy compliments soon escalated to I love you. That quickly became the determining factor for me to return home. I honestly had no idea what he was capable of. Over the years, my childhood pediatrician had become a mediator and liaison between my grandmother and me. So, before going home, I decided to speak to her. She always made time for me. I went to the hospital and she talked to me and my grandmother. I was going home.

Surprisingly, everything was good for a while. It wasn't too long before things went back to normal. It was time for a school dance and she decided that if I wanted to go, she was going to walk me there. Now imagine: me, all my friends and my grandmother, walking to the school dance. That wasn't going to happen, so I didn't go.

After some time passed, I got a phone call from the creepy guy from the drug house. Turned out that he had tricked my friend into giving him my number and address. A year later, he was stalking me, daily. One day he was sitting on the mailbox across from our apartment. He eventually rang the doorbell and asked if I lived there. Now just think of my grandmother as the Madea of our time. She was ruthless. She didn't take anything from anyone, and she could handle anyone.

My grandmother answered, "Yes, who wants to know?"

He walked away. He continued to drive around the complex for weeks. His next attempt at coming to the house brought him face to face with my uncle. My uncle had a long threatening conversation with him. After a year, I didn't hear from him. I figured it was over.

I regularly skipped school now, to hang out with my friends. One particular evening, I got a call from the school. There had been young gentleman who'd come to the school looking for me. My friend had seen him and had reported him. School security found him and to make a long story short, I'm glad I was absent that day—they found a weapon on him. He was arrested. I never heard from or about him again. You'd think going through this would make me never want to be on the streets again. Not so.

Fast-forward a bit. At 16 years old, I was a little more mature, but still very unhappy and still trying to win my grandmother's affection. I decided I wanted more freedom and the only way to achieve this was to graduate from school early and go to college. Not only was I no longer skipping school, I was going to day school, then straight to work at McDonalds, and then back to night school so that I could be a graduating junior. I had a 4.0 GPA in night school and a 3.5 GPA in day school. I had done a complete 180. Since I was doing so well, I asked my grandmother for a little more freedom. I asked for a curfew. I wanted to go out, dance with my friends and enjoy being a teen. Her answer was simply no! Graduating at 16 became even more appealing. But trouble was brewing and it had my name on it. I got into a fight that not only got me kicked me out of school, but landed me in court, with a court ordered curfew. Not the type of curfew I was looking for. One bad decision left me with a public defender whose only advice was to plead guilty. I kissed my Florida A&M future goodbye.

I was expelled from school and I went to work full time. I eventually moved out at 16 to live with friends. For a while, that worked until the morning I was awakened by the police who told me I had to leave. It was seven in the morning. Where was I going to go? I walked to another friend's house. Although she had two kids, she let me stay for a while, but I didn't want to overstay my welcome. I left to live with another friend and finally realized: this house-to-house situation had to end. Some nights, I'd walk around or sit on the porch all night. At sunrise, I would go to work.

After months of going house to house, I would return, once again, to my grandmother's house. This time for a month—less welcome, more attitude. I was working and going to night school. Some nights, I'd get a ride home from Todd, my boyfriend—there were more arguments and even more attitude. She didn't like Todd because he was so much older than I. But Todd and I had been friends since I was 13. In the end, she called the police on me one night and they made threats of sending me to boot camp. I politely, or maybe not so politely, informed the police officer that I was 16 and there was nothing he could do; I was moving out.

I worked full time at Wendy's and saved up enough money to move into my own place. I found a studio apartment, paid the security deposit and first month's rent all on my own. I went to an estate sale and purchased all of my furniture. To top it all off, the charges pending from eight months ago were dropped. Finally, I could see the road to freedom. I could get my life together, get my diploma and go to college, or so I thought.

My Pupa Stage

It was January 16, 1995. It was Martin Luther King, Jr. Day. I woke up sick and achy. Todd and I discussed the possibility of my being pregnant. This could not be happening! I was 17 years old, without a diploma, without a license, and working two part-time jobs. I was striving to get things back on track and now I was pregnant. I often found myself asking, "What am I going to do?"

Not only was the pregnancy unexpected, it was rough. I could not keep anything down. I was losing weight and I was weak all the time. I had to leave both jobs, move in with Todd and his mother, and rely on social services for assistance.

Todd was wonderful. Not once did he forsake his responsibilities as a father. If only he did not make music his life. He spent most of his time in the studio and was barely going to work. He was determined. I began to feel alone and ignored. I found a box of gospel tracks in his room and since I was on bed rest, I read them all. Reading those tracks put me on a journey with a new perspective on how I was going to raise our son, the things he would not be exposed to and the schooling he would receive.

June came and all of my friends graduated from high school. My best friend invited me to the ceremony. There I was, pregnant, congratulating all of my former classmates. I felt very discouraged. It was hard to envision a future for myself when I wasn't allowed to attend any school. To make matters worse, the looks and stares I received from adults cut like a knife. I just wanted to curl up in a corner and cry.

At eight and a half months, I could barely move. Todd and I were moving into what would be my third apartment. After the move, I was exhausted and swollen. I went to the hospital and they said it was normal but they kept me for observation. When I woke, I was surrounded by doctors explaining they were going to induce my labor. The baby was too big.

It was Labor Day and I was induced at nine in the morning

and ended up with a c-section at 12:25 am. I gave birth to a 9lb 15 oz. baby boy on September 5. The labor and the delivery were over but the pain did not cease. I had an infection and so did the baby. It would be two weeks before they discovered the sources. They had left fluid in my stomach from the c-section and my son had swallowed some of his bile during delivery.

Upon returning home four weeks later, I decided to give my life to the Lord. It was the best decision of my life but it didn't mean my hard journey as a teenage mother was over. At just eight weeks old, our son was rushed to the hospital with a fever that would not drop. I think the hardest, and scariest thing I had to do was watch them give my newborn baby a spinal tap to rule out meningitis. The results were negative, but the fever remained unchanged. After a couple of days, we prayed one last prayer over him, and by that evening his fever broke. Although the doctors could not explain why he was going through this, I knew it was to build our trust and faith in God as new believers. And it certainly did just that!

My Butterfly Stage

Realizing that our living situation or "shacking up" was not pleasing to God, Todd asked me to marry him. Of course, I said yes. I was excited about our little family. The only problem was I was 17. Since I lived on my own, I didn't think my grandmother would object to our marriage. She did and refused to sign the paperwork. So we waited and four days after my 18th birthday, we were married. Sadly, only four of my family members attended my wedding. My grandmother wasn't one of them. The rest of the attendees were close friends and Todd's family. Her absence on such an important day in my life, was very disappointing, but that was just one of many disappointments.

After getting married, I continued to struggle since I did not have my diploma and could not find decent employment. I was tired of working at Wendy's. I wanted to register for college classes to obtain my GED, but, without a car, it was almost impossible. I already had to take 4 buses in the morning and at night. Todd had reverted back to drinking, smoking weed and pursuing music. Later, we purchased a vehicle with our tax refund but issues arose. We argued and there were many times we just did not want to be together. He was putting music before his family and I felt like a single mom. Raising a family as a young mother, especially with the lack of finances was a struggle, but in 1998, there was a restoration in our faith and trust in God. We grew more, not only as a couple, but one with unshakable faith. Our struggle did not seem so hard to manage when walking wholeheartedly with the Lord.

Today, our son is now 17 and we are happily married. We have four beautiful children. I have my master's degree and I'm a successful executive and co-owner of a business with my husband. Most importantly, we love the Lord and each other more and more every day. At 17, my son is the same age I was when I gave birth to him. Although I used to be ashamed when asked how old I was, I do not regret bringing such an awesome, handsome, talented, and determined young man into the world. Although my life did not go as I had planned, it's going in the direction of God's perfect plan.

Although it would be easy to say if it were not for the way I was raised, then I would not be in the situation I'm in now, but I had choices to make. I chose not to make better decisions as a teen. But, just like a butterfly struggles to get out of its cocoon to fly, many times we have to go through our difficulties in order to be the beautiful people God has created us to be.

For the Lord disciplines those he loves, and he punishes each one he accepts as his child. Hebrews 12:6 NLT (©2007).

If it were not for him chastising me, I don't know how my life would have turned out.

Author's Corner

Biography: Charlyn Elliott is a columnist, inspirational writer, media, graphic and jewelry designer. She was born in Orlando, Florida, but was raised by her grandmother in Rochester, New York, where she currently resides. She earned a master's degree in media design from Full Sail University. Charlyn Elliott is the owner of Love Lynn's Designs and the Co-Owner of Todd E Media. When she's not writing, she enjoys spending time with her husband and four children who are the inspiration for her journey. The Journey of A Teenage Mother is her first co- authored book.

Acknowledgments: I would like to express great appreciation first and foremost to my Lord and Savior Jesus Christ for helping me through this great journey. Without Him none of this would be possible. I would like to acknowledge and thank my grandmother. If it were not for you I would have probably ended up in foster care. I appreciate you agreeing to take me in and raising me. I love you. Also to my wonderful husband, Todd T Elliott, Sr., who has been there from day one of my journey as a mother and has not forsaken his responsibilities. You have helped me grow as a wife, mother, and person and I love you more than words could express. I would like to offer my special thanks to my four beautiful children, Todd Jr., Tahjmere, Taliq, and Taleah. I love you all. You all inspire me in so many different ways to continue to move forward and to become a better person. My special thanks are extended to LaShunda Leslie Smith for allowing me to share my journey to encourage young ladies and women that there is hope. I thank you for being a pillar and for encouraging me to do more and be more. I love and appreciate you.

Contact Info:
Charlyn Elliott
www.charlynelliott.com
www.ilovelynns.com
charlyn@ilovelynns.com
Facebook: https://www.facebook.com/pages/
Love-Lynn-Designs/289651294386746
Twitter: @charlynelliott
Phone: 585-802-7818

TEN

THE QUIET STORM
LaToya Reaves

Growing up I dreamed of being a preacher, a choirmaster, and a musician. As time went on, I changed my dreams to becoming a lawyer since I thought I always had a valid argument. But becoming a teenage mother halted my pursuit of my dreams.

I was born to a teenage mother who gave birth to me two months after she graduated from high school. I didn't know my dad until I was much older. The Lord blessed me with another mother and family that cared and loved me like their own. I was raised with strong Christian morals and values. However, the parenting methods were different. I had one set of rules at home and another set with my adopted family. Sometimes the rules were very confusing. I was always closely monitored and not allowed to spend the night with friends. I went to private school through eighth grade.

In ninth grade, I experienced a real eye opener when I attended East High School. I was so out of my element. I didn't think I was pretty and I wasn't allowed to dress like the other kids, but I felt the need to try and fit in because of peer pressure. I wasn't exposed to the things my peers experienced. My friends were sexually active and were allowed to have boyfriends—it wasn't even a thought in my head. I was raised in a strong Christian home where sex was not talked about. The only thing my other mom said was not to do it until you were married. The messages were conflicting. With one family, it was no sex before marriage. With my other family, it was the norm to be a parent at a young age. I was academically above average and my conversations were about college and becoming a lawyer. My peers thought I was a nerd. My 3.27 G.P.A. dropped to a 1.09 by the end of my freshman year.

I met a guy who wanted to be my boyfriend. All my peers told me to leave him alone but I wanted to be cool. On January 20, 1995, I became pregnant with my daughter after my first sexual encounter. After missing my period, I remember going to the birthing center in Pittsford with my friend's sister who was also pregnant. The nurse told me I was six weeks pregnant. Fear, panic, anger, frustration and hopelessness, gripped me. I called my daughter's father to ask him how this happened when I'd seen him with the condom. He explained that he did it on purpose. All I could do was cry. I was in a daze. I was afraid to go home. I didn't know how I was going to take care of a baby because I wasn't old enough to even get a job. I knew that having an abortion wasn't an option. I called someone I thought was my friend from church to help me come up with a plan to tell my birth mom the news. She came right over to the house and we told my mom, but by Sunday, everyone at church also knew. My mother's reaction was shock and hurt. She didn't know how to respond. After getting my birth mom calmed down, I then had the task of calling my other mother. When I finally got the words out she was just very quiet. I instantly felt like a failure and was ashamed because I felt I had brought shame and embarrassment to my family. I felt like I let everyone down. I thought my life was over. Being a member of a pastor's family, people were more judgmental and cruel. I just had to learn to deal with it.

My birth mom wanted me to have an abortion because she felt I was too young to parent a child. She wanted me to finish school, go to college and to experience the things she couldn't as a teenage mom. My other mom offered to support me in whatever decision I made. I remember telling my aunt the news.

She looked at me and said, "It could have been AIDS. Thank God it's a baby!"

Her words gave me hope and inspiration. My birth mom took me to the doctor and they tried to talk me into having an abortion, but I refused. I was angry with my daughter's father because I felt he messed up my dreams. At the same time, I felt I finally had something that I could truly love and call my own.

Most of my church friends and their parents had a hard time with my being pregnant. They talked about me and wouldn't allow their kids to be around me, which hurt me more than anything. I stayed positive because I knew my baby had a purpose. My entire pregnancy was a battle between my mothers. My birth mom was still angry at my decision to have the baby and she was mad at my other mom for not agreeing with her. In the meantime, I suffered. I needed and wanted my birth mom to tell me what to expect and guide me on this life changing journey. She didn't.

When I was five months pregnant, I was sitting next to my grandfather when my baby kicked for the first time. I was so scared I jumped up and ran to my room. I didn't know what it was and I panicked. At my next doctor's appointment, I talked with my doctor and she explained what was happening inside me. My other mom and my daughter's godmother gave me a small baby shower when I was 8 months pregnant, which my birth mother didn't attend. Again, it was painful to accept.

In my ninth month, the anticipation to see my baby, along with other questions in my head like how would I know if I were in labor, were weighing me down. By mid–October, I was ready for it to all be over. I became restless and very moody. I had a home tutor who came for 2 hours every day. I was bored out of my mind but still excited that my baby would soon be here. On October 25, 1995, I went to my OB appointment and the doctor told me that I was still one cm dilated. I told her that I would see her on Saturday, the 28th, because that was my due date. She said you have to be in labor.

I said, "Oh, I will be, trust me."

When my appointment was over, my other mother decided that we were going to walk around Irondequoit Mall.

After walking for about an hour I told her that it felt like my bones were separating.

She said, "Keep walking. I am going to walk this baby out of you."

We finally left the mall and she rewarded me with Applebee's. I will never forget it. It was an all you can eat rib night. I ate so much that they had to pull the table out to let me up. I was happy and full, but that pain was still in my back. My other mom took me to Tops and had me walking up and down every aisle. I couldn't take it anymore and was glad when I finally made it home. On October 26, 1995, at about 5:00 a.m., I started having contractions. Since I didn't understand what was happening, I just thought I needed to use the restroom. I tried to lie down after I couldn't go to the restroom, but at about 6:00 a.m., I was back in the bathroom. This time the urge was even stronger. After about 45 minutes, my grandfather told my grandmother to come check on me.

"Get up before you have the baby in the toilet!" She yelled.

I called my other mom and told her what was going on. My birth mom laid in her bed until my grandparents made her get up. She called the doctor at about 9:00 a.m. and they told her to bring me in. My grandfather had to make her go with me. When we got to the hospital, my grandmother helped me get ready for delivery while my birth mom stayed in the restroom. I was dilated 7 centimeters when the doctor checked me. I couldn't get any pain meds and the pain was unbearable. I called my daughter's father, but he wasn't home. My other mother was on her way and it was time to push. I refused to push until she came through the door. As soon as she came thru the door and grabbed one leg while my grandmother held the other, I began to push and my beautiful bundle of joy was born at 11:27 a.m. She weighed 6lbs 8oz. Looking down at my beautiful, healthy baby, whom I had carried inside me, was the best feeling I ever felt in my life. I knew that all the walking from the night before had paid off.

My other mom stayed with me the first night. She helped me fill out paperwork and taught me how to hold and feed my baby. The second night, I was alone thinking about my goals and plans, nervous about being a good mom and wondering how I was going to provide for my baby. When it was time for discharge, my birth mom came to pick me up. Being home was scary for me because I didn't know what to expect. My birth mom was living her life and not ready to accept the responsibilities of being a grandmother. She told me that she wasn't babysitting to make it easier for me to have another baby. My grandmother helped me at night when my baby woke up. My other mom came to visit every day until I was able to walk outside and helped me to get my first job at Wendy's. When my baby was two months old, my other mom told me my baby was my responsibility and I had to provide for her. She also said that welfare wasn't an option and I needed to learn to save and continue my education to make more money.

I went back to school when my baby was 3 months old. My aunt watched her for me. I was focused in all of my classes because I knew I had to be an example for my daughter. I refused to be a statistic and so I used everyone's negativity to keep me motivated. When my baby was eight months old, my other mother decided to move away to continue her education. I was hurt and devastated. Without her, I feared the unknown. She was my everything and I never imagined life without her. My aunt and cousin stepped right in and helped me in any way they could.

My birth mom finally moved out from my grandparent's house when I was 17. My grandmother forced me to go because she said it was time for my birth mom to have her own responsibility as a parent. She was in a relationship with a man who I didn't get along with, so I was forced to move in with my aunt and her children. I still went to school, took my daughter to daycare and worked at Wendy's. I graduated from East High School in June of 1997.

After graduation, I worked two jobs to provide for myself and my daughter. I eventually moved in with an elderly aunt when plans to move in with my birth mom fell apart. She taught me so much and always encouraged me to keep going and press my way. She prayed with me and on my rough days she always seemed to have the right words to say. In the spring of 1998, I registered to be a student at MCC. I was unsure of what I wanted to do because I had buried my dreams. I made the dean's list my first semester.

When I was 19 years old, I fell into a deep depression that lasted several years. My daughter was 3 years old when I had my first episode. After that, I was in and out of the hospital. My family, especially my mom, grandmother, aunts, and my daughter's godmother, helped me with my daughter. Her father moved to Atlanta when she was 4 and didn't have much contact with her. When she was 6, I went to live in a group home for 8 months. I went home on the weekends. As a mother, I felt horrible. My daughter was parentless and I was a bad parent. But, I kept fighting and trying to do better. During my healthy times, I instilled the importance of education and gave her all of my time.

At age 7, she developed a love for the game of basketball. I enrolled her in community leagues followed by the Boys and Girls club. I was fighting mental illness but I was determined to keep my baby's dreams alive. Her father, on the other hand, wanted to take my dreams away. He waited until I was healthy and stable and then fought me for custody when she was 8 years old. My baby was my key to survival. I fought to live for her and I couldn't afford to lose her. Eventually, I was awarded sole custody.

I enrolled my daughter in a suburban school where she continued to excel at playing basketball. She was traveling and playing competitively. I made sacrifices to pay for hotels and travel every weekend, because I knew she was gifted. I wanted her to have the best education, so again I made a sacrifice. I sent her to private school in 8th grade. She told me she wanted to go to college to be a pharmacist and I began nurturing that seed.

Life seemed to be going great until I had another bout with depression. Only this time I was trying to self medicate with alcohol. Nothing improved until I fully accepted the fact that depression was an illness. I began to work with healthcare professionals which helped me to get better and I was able to get it under control.

The stigma associated with mental illness hinders people from being open or talking about it. Despite my history of depression, I decided to go back to school. In 2007, I enrolled in Finger Lakes Community College to work on my RN. I wanted my daughter to see me accomplish my goal. I graduated with my AS in liberal arts while working. On graduation day, I was so proud of myself! Seeing my family happy made me ecstatic.

"Mom, I always believed in you. I am so proud of you. You are my role model."

When my daughter said these words, I cried. She gave me new hope and strength.

I began classes at Roberts Wesleyan for my baccalaureate degree, but due to my daughter's rigorous schedule and my parenting responsibilities, I decided to postpone my classes until after she completed high school.

During this time, I was invited to be on the Department of Psychiatry Consumer Advisory Board at Strong Hospital. I received the opportunity to educate myself and work with psychiatrists, med students, nurses, and other mental health workers about how to improve care for the mentally ill and help break the stigma associated with the illness. This proved to be very rewarding.

In my daughter's junior year, we started discussing her college choices and the possibility of relocating to give us both a change. The opportunity presented itself and we moved with my aunt and her children to Los Angeles, CA for her senior year. My daughter was always a popular child which didn't change when we moved across the country. She joined the basketball team and made friends and said this was the best decision we made in our lives. Life was less stressful and we had much more time to connect.

Today, she is graduating and heading to college to pursue a degree as a pharmacist. I am proud of her. Now that she is moving on to college, I am going to pursue my goals of furthering my education. I will also want to continue to advocate for the mentally ill.

I am grateful to God for all that I endured during my experience as a teen mom. The task wasn't easy, but God knew I would make it thru. It made me stronger and proud to know that I beat the statistics and raised a successful child that is headed to college.

Author's Corner

Biography: LaToya Reaves was born and raised in Rochester, New York. She is the proud parent of one daughter. LaToya received her A.S. in liberal arts from Finger Lakes Community College. LaToya was a volunteer for the University of Rochester Department of Psychiatry Patient Advisory Board where she has advocated and given speeches to doctors, health care professionals, med students, and others in the community about mental health stigmas and awareness. LaToya currently lives in Los Angeles, California, and is looking to continue her education in nursing and psychology.

Acknowledgments: I would like to thank God first and foremost for giving me the strength and courage to handle being a teen mom. To my baby, Teja, you are my world. I am proud to be your mom and love you very much. To my mothers, Sonya and Carmelitta, thanks for everything you have both instilled in me. Without the both of you I wouldn't be who I am today. I am grateful that God chose you both to be my mothers. I love you both more than you will ever know. To my grandparents, Ella and the late Henry Reaves, I appreciate the both of you. You both were babysitters while I went to school and worked. Thanks for providing me with a stable place to live with my baby. Most of all, thanks for instilling the importance of prayer and making God the head of my life. To Grand mommy, Dr. Eulah M. Nelson, and Granddaddy, Eld. I.V. Nelson, thanks for teaching me and showing me that I can handle any task that is given to me. Even in my lonely moments you always had a word to lift me up. I have utilized the faith that you showed me. Thanks for the Godly morals and values that you taught and instilled in me. To all my aunts, especially Aunt Shelli, Aunt Sara,

Aunt Pamela, and Auntie Dita, thanks for all your help and support. You all know how important you are to me. To my daughter's godmother, Johnitta, thanks for stepping in when needed and guiding me in the task of being a young mother. I made the best choice by choosing you. To my little cousin/sister Alexis, thanks for being my babysitter and for all of the sacrifices you made. To my big cousin, Jamie, thanks for being an important male figure in my life and teaching me how a lady is supposed to be treated. To my girl Kaye-Kaye, you've stuck with me through my entire pregnancy until now. Thanks for being a true friend. In memory of Aunt Vivian and Aunt Ella, my angels, I wish you were here to see that I made it. To the staff at Strong Memorial Hospital, especially Deb Maimone, Lisa Dennison, Teri Diguiseppe, Rita Moore, and Caroline Nestro, thanks for believing in me and pushing me through the dark storm into my destiny.

Contact Info:
LaToya Reaves
toyareaves@gmail.com
Facebook: https://www.facebook.com/latoya.reaves.3

ELEVEN

ENDURED IT ALL
Shenita Harper

I was always told the famous line of do as I say and not as I do. This was the statement I remember the most while growing up in a single parent household down in the Mississippi Delta. In elementary and junior high school, I was involved in a lot of extracurricular activities and I was a good student academically. My freshman year in high school things started to change and I mean at a fast pace. I have the kind of family that feels as if everyone must know what is going on with everyone. I did not feel as if I could confide in anyone with regards to my inner feelings. No one ever talked to me about a menstrual cycle, virginity, and all the things that girls go through, including handling boys. I learned some things from health in school and the many pamphlets that were handed out. A lot of things I learned by taking risks and dealing with the consequences that followed.

I think that every individual has a purpose in life. I must admit that I had a self-esteem issue because of my weight. I was always the fat girl amongst my peers, or those whom I called friends at the time. It is a hurtful feeling when you know you are not accepted by certain people, including family. I thought fat girls could not get a boyfriend. I didn't think about keeping my mind on my studies and worrying about boys later on in life. My father has always been a part of my life, but he wasn't able to give me what I needed him the most for during my teen years. The teen years are when a father, or father figure, is needed to tell a girl she is beautiful no matter what. I really hate to think about this. I often asked myself who really loves me for me? That is a question that I still find myself trying to answer.

A couple of months into my freshman year of high school I noticed this tall, dark, stocky male in the school cafeteria. At that time, I thought he was the most handsome guy I had ever seen. A couple of friends introduced us and we just kind of hit it off from that point forward. We exchanged phone numbers and talked on a consistent basis. He was a football player and my mother allowed him to come over some days after practice. We began to visit more often at each other's homes. At this point, I did not realize that I was in a full blown relationship with this young man.

I am not sure if my mother had noticed a change in me, but for some reason she stated that I needed to make an appointment to see a doctor. I thought she was going to have one of my aunts take me like they had done before, but this time was different. As we were waiting to be called back into the doctor's office after having taken a pregnancy test, my mother questioned me about the two lines on the pregnancy test. I told her that I did not know why mine had two lines. Well, to both of our surprise, one day before my 15th birthday, I was told I was pregnant. I just sat stiff with a lump in my throat not knowing how to tell the young man. After school that day I broke the news to him. I also told him that I did not have an option per my mother, I was to have an abortion. He was not upset about my being pregnant, but was about the fact that my mother was considering making me have an abortion. He told his mother, and both of our parents met and talked about the situation. Not only was it a surprise to find out I was pregnant, but I was shocked to find out that my child's father was not a junior, but a senior headed to a community college to play football. His mother made it quite clear that he was going off to college. She also said that she did not believe in abortions and did not want anything to do with that.

I was very close to my mother's youngest sister, who now is deceased. I was able to talk to her and she told my grandmother about my situation. As I explained earlier, there are no family secrets, everybody knows it all. Being the third generation as a teen mom was a hard pill to swallow. My mother cried and stated that she wanted me to break the cycle, not to continue it. Not only were we all teens, we were all 15 when we gave birth. It really hurt me so badly that my mother considered an abortion for me, but instead, she thought she might send me away to live with relatives until after I had had the baby. I guess I was an embarrassment to her. Remember my first sentence, do as I say not as I do.

I returned to school after my summer vacation with a baby bump. I continued to attend school until I gave birth to a healthy baby boy, on December 13, 1997. I had family support from my mother and my paternal family as well. My paternal grandmother has always supported me from an infant through present. I can honestly say, through her prayers and faith, I am continuously blessed. I continued to care for my son throughout my high school years. At the age of 16, I was able to obtain a part-time job after school. My mother assisted me with caring for the baby during those hours, as well as on the weekends. I had very minimum help from my son's father, which caused us to discontinue our relationship.

So there I was, a high school student, working, and caring for an infant. The struggle is real, was real, so I cannot sit here and say that it was all peaches and cream. There were plenty of nights I had to stay up with a sick baby while trying to do homework. As time progressed, I was still able to attend school functions and excel academically. I was able to graduate a semester early because I had completed all of the necessary requirements for graduation. As I walked across the stage and began to exit, I heard a familiar voice that was crying for his momma. Exiting the building, diploma in one hand and my baby in my arms, I was crying tears of joy. Being the great-granddaughter of a sharecropper has always been stuck in my head. I wanted to be above all of that and to make my family proud no matter what. I had dreams of one day becoming a registered nurse. I never wanted to be known as a statistic because I was a teen parent. I always felt that I could overcome any barrier and not let having a baby at a young age determine the course of my future.

At the age of 17, in January 2000, I was enrolled as a college freshman. I was excited because I knew that I had accomplished graduating from high school and there were more goals to set. I got the opportunity to live on campus and experience life as a college student. My mother allowed me that opportunity by taking care of my son, but things just did not feel the same leaving my baby at home with my mom. I did not want to be labeled as having abandoned my baby or as putting my responsibilities off on someone else. After my first semester, my mother purchased me a car so I could travel home to visit my son, but I was responsible for paying the car payments. Prior to getting the car, my mind was set on finding employment because I wanted to get a place for myself and my son. I was hired as a summer employee with the federal government. I did some research and learned that the government allowed college students to work year round if there was a position available. A closed mouth does not get fed, so I presented that information to the scientist that I worked for and she hired me for a year round position. I continued to work in that position throughout all four years of college. At the age of 19, I continued to work and attend college. I decided that I no longer wanted to stay on the university campus. I was able to get an apartment for my son and myself even though the commute to campus was forty-five minutes.

As I mentioned earlier, my mother's youngest sister was someone very close to me. In 2001, she was diagnosed with pancreatic cancer. She was given six months to live. In between raising my son, I also had the responsibility of helping with her two small children. She passed away in January, 2002, at the age of 28. It devastated me to see her go through so much pain and suffering. Through all of the hurt from her death, I still continued to pray and work even harder.

I continued my studies at the university while working and providing for my son. My son often visited with my family during the weekends which gave me an opportunity to hang out with friends. Well, in the midst of hanging out, I met this guy who was 10 years my senior. I had seen him in passing, but other than that it was nothing. We exchanged numbers and started to hang out. As time progressed we continued to see each other. Of course, I know what you are thinking, here she goes again. After a few months, I became pregnant but had a miscarriage. That should have been my sign to just keep it moving forward and to deal with this guy from a distance. This guy was a well-known individual in my small hometown, so it was a lot that came with that coal black hair and smooth chocolate skin of his. Everything that looks good is not always good for you. I was in for a ride with this one and did not know it. I should have learned from the first boy in my life, just because you have sex with someone does not mean he loves you. That was what I needed my father to explain to me, but it never happened.

In my senior year of college, I was pregnant with my second child. I did not have a good relationship with the second father, nor did I know any of his family. I just felt as if I really did not know him. He is what you'd call a street man, called so because of the type of lifestyle he lived. I can be honest and say that all money is not good money. The saying all that glitters is not gold is very true. I guess I was looking for love in all of the wrong places. I continued to work throughout my pregnancy and continued my studies. On July 10, 2003, at the age of 21, I gave birth to a healthy baby who I call my baby girl. Things were really hard because I now had two mouths to feed with no support from either father. On December 13, 2003, which was also my son's 6th birthday, I graduated from college with a bachelor of science in family and consumer sciences (consumer relations) with a minor in office administration. My daughter was five months old at the time. I was able to breastfeed her and I felt that we had a bond and were inseparable. I was praying that we could make it through the ceremony without a loud outburst from her. I was very anxious and excited to walk across that stage. I knew that I had done something that no one in my immediate family had done. That made me feel proud knowing that I had beaten the odds with not one, but two children.

Where do I go from here was the big question. There I was raising two children with no support from either father. I knew there had to be a better way. In March, 2004, during my son's spring break from school, I decided to take a trip to visit family in Las Vegas, Nevada. I had not been to Las Vegas since 1992 and of course a lot had changed. I was able to tour the city and to see what kind of employment opportunities were available. After dealing with the second father and all of his shenanigans, I decided I needed a change from Mississippi. Just because an individual is grown in age does not mean they are grown in maturity. He was not grown.

I decided it was time for me to step out and test my faith. I had constantly prayed and asked God for guidance and to give me strength to continue to raise my babies. So, after returning from the spring trip, I started packing and shipping all of my belongings to Las Vegas. I was able to store everything in my relative's garage. I purchased two plane tickets, and in May of 2004, I stepped out on faith and never looked back with any regrets. I was blessed to live with my relatives for a whole year until I gained stable employment. During that year, I purchased things such as furniture and other items for an apartment. Prior to moving into my own place, God blessed me with a brand new vehicle. I was working as a library assistant with the summer months off. I had no idea how I would be able to afford the vehicle or the apartment, but I was blessed with a summer position until the regular school year started again. I continued to apply for positions within the school district and government agencies. I was blessed again with my current position a family support specialist, with the local child support office, where I have now been for eight years. My family continued to help me with my children. I made a promise to myself that I was moving to Las Vegas for change, not to work in a hotel and make beds. I was determined and very persistent. Once I graduated with my bachelor's degree, I did not have the desire to attend school again. But, working in a government agency, the opportunity to work towards a master's degree was presented to employees. In January of 2008, I enrolled into the master's program. My children were 4 years old and 10 years old. I constantly reminded myself that I was doing this for my children; I had to think about their future. I stayed in the program, but my mind shifted gears. I had to change my living situation because my kids were getting older and needed separate bedrooms. I stepped out in faith once again. I had just traded in my first car and got another one, so I was thinking my credit should be decent enough to apply for a home mortgage. In April, 2009, the day before my birthday, I was not signing papers in a doctor's office about a pregnancy, I was signing the documents for my new home. That was the greatest gift of all, to be able to provide a home for my children. I have been very determined to accomplish goals that I have set and I can rejoice now that life is all working out.

In May of 2011, I walked the stage once again to be awarded a certificate in public management and a master's in public administration. I know that you are probably thinking, or may want to say, that is enough schooling. In my opinion, you are never too old to learn and there is always room for growth. I am blessed that I have a job, though I think there is more to come. I am continuing to raise my children and work full-time. Presently, I am enrolled in a doctoral program pursing my PhD in general human services. I am not quite sure what my future holds in regards to my career, but I am sure I will be able to use every degree I earn.

Once upon a time I thought I had to prove something to people because I was a teen parent. I am done proving anything to anyone. What I have learned over the years is that people will talk about you if you are doing good or bad. As long as I have confidence within myself I do not have to prove anything to anybody. I have overcome several obstacles in life. I made a promise to myself to let go of individuals who only speak negativity and who lack respect for me and my accomplishments. I also stand tall and speak loudly and clearly that it is okay for me to raise my kids as a single parent because I made the choice to have them. I may cry sometimes, but it only makes me stronger. I have been taking my responsibilities seriously for almost 16 years and I am not ashamed to say the struggle is real. But, my children believe in me and I believe in me. Nothing beats a failure but a try, and I will continue to try, try, and try again. What I can say to be true is that once you write down a goal or a dream, if you pray, believe, speak it into existence, and work hard, it will all fall into place according to God's plan.

Author's Corner

Biography: Shenita Harper earned a bachelor of science in family and consumer sciences with a concentration in consumer relations and a minor in office administration from Delta State University, located in Cleveland, Mississippi, in December of 2003. After relocating to Las Vegas, Nevada, she was employed as a family support specialist working with the local child support office. The opportunity was presented to further her education through her employer in collaboration with The University of Nevada, Las Vegas. She then enrolled in The Graduate Certificate in Public Management Program and earned a certificate in public management in December of 2008. After receiving her certificate, she was able to apply for the master's program that following year. In May, 2011, Shenita graduated from The University of Nevada, Las Vegas, with her master's in public administration. As she continues to strive hard in being successful and looking for future employment opportunities, she refuses to stop and just settle. In September, 2011, Shenita enrolled in a doctoral program at Capella University where she is pursuing her doctoral degree in general human services. She is eager to learn new things and is always looking for an opportunity to grow. She is also a mandated court appointed special advocate (CASA) for abused and neglected children who are in the foster care system. She attends The Greater Mt. Sinai Missionary Recruiting Ministries, Incorporated in Las Vegas, Nevada. She is a believer and thinks that all things happen for a reason and believes one should always have faith. Shenita has not taken this journey alone. She has been blessed with two children, Anthony and Tariyonna.

Acknowledgments: I give thanks to God, because without Him, nothing is possible. To my children, Anthony and Tariyonna, you are the reason for everything I do. Without you two, I do not know what my life would be. To my mother, Jackie, you made it all possible in the very beginning by giving me that opportunity that so many others wish they could have had. To my sister, Chiquita, thanks for your words of inspiration. I truly take them to heart. To my grandmother, Ludella, thanks for being the praying woman you are. You have always instilled in me that prayer changes things and that one cannot live without it. You also helped me learn patience by teaching me that everything happens on God's time and not my time. To my Aunt Tracy, no, I didn't forget you... thanks, because you have been there from the beginning as well. To my Las Vegas family, thank you because you gave me that opportunity to step out in faith! To Lamont, all I can say is thanks for being a best friend and listening to me when no else is listening. To my sister-friend Laura, I love you and you are truly a blessing in my life. I am thankful to God for the following women because not only are they friends, but they are more like family...Deana, Linda, Mary, Vivian, and Delerrie. Thank you all for believing in me and your continuous support throughout my journey.

Contact Info:
Shenita Harper
www.letstalkinspiration.com
info@letstalkinspiration.com
Facebook: https://www.facebook.com/mssuchaqt
Phone: 702-625-1736

TWELVE

PLAY THE HAND YOU HAVE BEEN GIVEN
Rosa M. Day

Some people, about to become parents for the first time, are excited because they have waited and hoped for an addition to their family. Others, for whom parenthood wasn't a goal, may be afraid, angry, bewildered, and confused, wondering how their life will change. They may wonder, *What if I am not a good parent?, or, I never wanted a child; I am not ready.* Regardless of the emotion, pregnancy is the time when the entrance of someone new into our lives affects our world.

My story begins with my parents who were considered to be middle class. My father worked as a polisher at an optical manufacturer and my mother as a seamstress at a company that manufactured suits for men and boys. I have three brothers, Joseph, the oldest, Nelson, the middle, and Jeffery, the baby. I am the second to the oldest. During the 1970's, many of the African Americans I knew were experiencing some form of abuse in the home. My dad was a good provider financially for the family, but he had an explosive personality and was a functioning alcoholic. According to our family's definition, a functioning alcoholic is one that works every day, but drinks to the point of drunkenness every evening. Dad didn't display much physical abuse; his method of abuse was primarily mental. He would intimidate us with objects and threaten to beat us into submission. There was a lot of arguing in our home. He was the only one participating in the arguments. Most of my dad's explosive episodes were based on unfounded accusations of infidelity that he hurled at my mom and they were predicated by an enormous amount of alcohol. Gin was his demon of choice.

One of these episodes occurred after my dad had worked all day, had purchased and drunk his gin, and had gone to bed early to sleep it off. We all knew not to wake him up prior to him getting all of his sleep, because he would be meaner than usual. However, my uncle who was visiting, did not know this. Larry, my boyfriend at the time, had come over to pick me up to celebrate the New Year. After meeting Larry, my uncle who at times would antagonize situations, slipped upstairs, woke my dad up and asked him of Larry's identity. Dad exploded. He began accusing mom of having a man in the house while he slept; he pushed, cursed, and threatened her. I thought that I could mitigate the situation by talking to Dad. There were times I could divert his attention by getting him to talk about when he was a child in North Carolina. I had hoped to calm him down; it did not work. Dad began swinging at me; I swung back. The irony of the situation was that my uncle was nowhere to be found. Mom urged me out of the house, and I stayed the night with an aunt (who also lived with an abusive husband). The next day my brother told me that dad had gone to my room with a lead pipe that evening looking for me.

My mother on the other hand was docile and had a very forgiving nature. Mom spent much of her time ensuring that we were cared for. She worked a forty hour job, like my father, but also had the added responsibility of cooking, cleaning, ensuring that the bills were paid, running the house, and attempting to get her four children through high school unmarred by pregnancy, drugs, or jail. Mom never talked to us about dad's out breaks of anger, even when we were begging her to leave him. Dad's behavior and mom's passive acceptance of his aggression left my brothers and me with what we termed as knots in our stomach. We were afraid of our father when he was drinking, because we never knew who, when, or what would set him off. We also knew that he had been a semi-professional boxer when he was younger. Once, before our eyes, he had killed someone in self-defense. He was the law in our home and, right or wrong, we had to follow it or leave.

Regardless, our parents loved us, but mom primarily interacted with us. Dad's limited involvement included financially supporting the family, administering corrective discipline to the children and annually taking us to North Carolina to visit our grandparents. Also, there were few expectations placed on us related to college or academic advancement, other than we must graduate from high school. But, I desired to further my education.

In June of 1977, I fulfilled my academic requirement by graduating from high school. Immediately, I began looking for employment. After months of looking for a job, I finally found seasonal employment at Sibley's department store as a gift wrapper. My job at Sibley's ended on Christmas Eve, so I was back to looking for permanent employment.

I enjoyed dancing and had begun going to various local clubs on the weekend. On September 17, 1977, at the Club Caribbean, I met the previously mentioned Larry. I was seventeen and he was four years older than I and had a car. Larry and I quickly began an unhealthy on again off again relationship which was comprised of immature arguments. In my opinion, Larry was fascinating; he worked for Gleason Works and seemed to have a career path. I later found out that he also had a path that included the company of many young ladies and that he had a child, a beautiful little girl. Our relationship quickly escalated and ultimately led to sexual intimacy by the following year.

Then it happened! One of the pivotal points in my life was Wednesday, February 22 ,1978. My youngest brother, four years my junior, and I were fighting. He threw a toss pillow at me and the corner hit me in the eye. I was so enraged I wanted to kill him. My personality had always been a mix of my parents; my dad's side was only displayed on rare occasions when I was pushed. I wondered why I let a pillow fight move me to such anger? I wasn't sure if my hormones, PMS or some other changes in me were triggering this sudden rage. I was reminded that my last menstrual cycle was January 12th and I still had not seen my period. Although I briefly entertained the idea of being pregnant, I really didn't think that it could happen to me. To soothe my conscience, I made a doctor's appointment for 9:30 am on March 6, 1978, hoping that I wasn't pregnant.

It felt like I was having an out of body experience, when the doctor told me I was pregnant. During this time, the option of aborting the child was presented. Larry and I were not currently on speaking terms and yet I was pregnant with his child. My father had always said that if I got pregnant, I would have to leave the house. The thought of having nowhere to live and being pregnant was more than I could bear. Larry called the following day and I told him that I was pregnant, we were not sure what we were going to do; however, we knew we would not abort the child. That day, and throughout the evening, my mind was filled with the fact that I was eighteen, pregnant, unemployed, under educated, in an unstable relationship, and possibly homeless. Within weeks my mother was asking me if I were pregnant. First, I evaded the conversation, but when asked again, I confessed. Mom assured me that she would help me; her comfort was more than I could have hoped for. My April 5th doctor's appointment confirmed that I was 10 - 12 weeks along with a due date around the end of October, 1978.

I still had not told my father and was afraid of his reaction. The time had come to tell him. It was a cold, Sunday morning in April.

I said, "Dad, I am pregnant."

He was very calm and told me that he knew this would happen and that everything he said came to pass. I left home and went to stay with my oldest brother and his fiancé; I didn't want to give dad the chance to kick me out. Larry asked me to marry him or to at least move in with him. Although I felt that I loved him, I did not trust him. Larry went and talked to my father, paving the way for another conversation between dad and me; it went well. Dad expressed his disappointment, but told me his home was always my home and that I was his daughter. We hugged and cried. I returned home.

I went to the Department of Social Services (DSS) to attempt to get assistance and was told that I was considered a minor and that my parents must take care of me until I turned twenty-one. DSS would not provide any financial assistance. They also informed me that if my parents kicked me out of the house, they would take my parents to court and make them support me. I was so discouraged. Later that month, my mom went with me to DSS and they told us they could not help us. Upon walking out with tears in my eyes because my decision had placed my parents in this financially tough situation, a woman stopped us and told me that although they would not cover me, they would cover my unborn child. I applied for my child, who began receiving assistance, $75 dollars a month. I had to budget, but that was enough money to assist with the purchase of the crib, clothes, diapers, milk and other essentials.

I continued to look for employment, but could not find a job. In May, I decided to apply to Manpower, which later became Rochester Career Skills Center, a trade school providing clerical training. I passed the entrance exam and was told that I would begin classes on June 19th. I was so excited. However, ten days before I was to start classes, during my orientation, they discovered that I was pregnant. I was then told that I would not be able to start school until after the baby was born. The reason I was given was that it would be a strain on me and the baby. I could not secure a job, because I was pregnant; I could not go to school, because I was pregnant.

The summer of 1978 was extremely hot. This, coupled with

alcohol, seemed to lead dad to become excessively violent. On one occasion, he pointed a knife at my mother. I told him I would kill him if he hurt her. He told me to leave; I did. My home was not the ideal setting for a stress free pregnancy but it was all I had, or thought that I had. I stayed with my oldest brother again until I heard that dad might have had a religious experience. Dad's religious experience lasted three months. As we entered September, it was filled with events such as my baby shower and helping to plan my brother's wedding and reception. I felt all alone and had to combat moments of depression. Most of my girlfriends were pregnant, or had just had a child, and all of our situations were fairly similar. We were teenage moms in unhealthy relationships. We didn't understand the importance of commitment in relationships, so we accepted unfaithfulness and beatings.

I desperately wanted to move out of my parent's house, but my financial situation would not allow me to adequately support my child. Dad continued arguing. Larry continued to be irresponsible and to not contribute financially to the welfare of our child. I took odd jobs babysitting for our neighbor or for family members for $20 a week. It wasn't much, but my options were slim. After a few weeks of babysitting for my neighbor, she lost her job. I was unemployed once again. One of my girlfriends, Carolyn, gave me a baby shower. The major items I needed for the child I received from the shower or I had saved for or had placed on lay-away. Also, my mother, my oldest brother and his fiancé, and my aunt were all a big help in providing me with some of the essentials for my baby.

I thought that if I had a girl, I would name her Nakisha,

which means unconquered. If I had a boy, the name would be Darnel, Larry's middle name. I continued to go to my doctors' appointments and I changed my eating habits. Prior to the pregnancy, I did not eat a healthy diet. I attended childbirth classes in anticipation of this new life. As it got closer to the end of October, I became restless and aggravated; there was no baby and no signs of a baby coming soon. Finally, on October 31st ,I had contractions ten minutes apart all day, but by the end of the day, there was still no baby. November 1st came and there were periodic contractions, but again, no baby. On Thursday, November 2, 1978, I woke up at 4 am with contractions that were five minutes apart, it was time. After waiting an hour before waking my parents, we headed to the hospital. The doctors thought that it was false labor because I had only dilated 2 centimeters and they were going to send me home. Within a short period of time, I had a bloody show which was an indicator that I was in labor. I told my mother to hold my hand and that I didn't want to scream like the other ladies I had heard through-out the maternity ward. It didn't take long after the bloody show for the contractions to be more pronounced and the dilation to increase rapidly. I started pushing at 3:00 pm and was taken to the delivery room. After four pushes, at 3:31 pm, I had Nakisha Janine. She weighed 6lbs, 3oz and was 20 ½ inches long. She was the most beautiful child I had ever seen, and I instantly loved her. Labor was the most uncomfortable feeling. It felt like a mix of cramps and bad gas pains. My mother was there with me throughout the pregnancy, labor, and delivery Without her, I might have panicked.

I shared my hospital room with a lady named Sheila. Her

baby was sick and died of pneumonia and a fatal heart condition. I recall feeling this overwhelming thought that my baby was going to die. Larry visited us at the hospital and thought that Nakisha was beautiful, but he had wanted a boy.

On November 24th, three weeks after Nakisha' s birth, she had a temperature of 102^0. I called the doctor and was told that based on her age, her temperature was too high and it could fry her brain. I freaked out and began crying uncontrollably. My thoughts went instantly to Sheila and her baby and I thought I would lose Nakisha. She was admitted into the hospital so that tests could be run. She was strapped down and had various IV's running. Her diagnosis was inconclusive. I took her home four days later. Having Nakisha, fondly known as Kisha, further motivated me to continue moving forward in my life.

By the end of November, I had scheduled an appointment with Rochester Career Skills Center to begin school, and started January 8, 1979. I had secured childcare with two of my great-aunts and would also use the help of my younger brothers when they were out of school. I didn't have transportation, nor could I drive, so I caught the bus to my great-aunt Annie's house on Tremont, then caught the bus to get to school on West Main Street. Rochester Career Skills Center provided two hundred hours of training in accounting, typing, and filing. I thought these classes would prepare me for the business world. I graduated from Rochester Career Skills Center in May 1979, with a certificate as an accounting clerk.

I also had begun to sporadically attend various churches and to have Bible studies in our home with the Jehovah Witnesses. Although I didn't know much about the Bible, nor did I know many Christians, I felt that the root of the Jehovah Witness belief system was not for me. On April 1, 1979, my life changed forever. I accepted Jesus Christ into my life to be my Lord and Savior while attending Church of the First Born. The church was located around the corner from where my parents lived, so it made it convenient to attend services. The change process was gradual, but constant. I began reading my Bible and praying. I began to feel more alive.

I still had not found a job, but on April 20, 1979, due to the humiliating and dehumanizing process of social services, I took Kisha off all services except Medicaid. I was unsure as to how to apply my training; therefore, I continued to fill out applications for employment. Rite Aid pharmacy was the first company that offered me a job. I started working there in July of 1979 as a cashier. In October of 1979, Central Trust Company (later acquired by M&T Bank), a locally operated bank ,offered me a position as a proof operator and I accepted the position while I continued to work at Rite Aid until January of 1980.

As a proof operator at Central Trust Company, my work day was from 1:00 pm to 10:00 pm. This job taught me the importance of deadlines and of personal discipline. At the age of nineteen, I had to juggle the responsibilities of being a single teen mother caring for my daughter with that of working two jobs and growing my new found faith. My job consisted of encoding 1,500 deposits and checks and ensuring that they balanced. After a year as a proof operator, I transferred into the micrographics department, where I researched customer's requests. After a year and a half, I transferred into the trust department. The trust department handled investments, taxes, administrative support and operational services to clients who maintained accounts with a minimum trust balance of one quarter of a million dollars. I started as a group leader of the trust data processing department and within a year, I became the supervisor of the department. The trust department gave me my first glimpse into corporate America and how to run a business. I became interested in climbing the corporate ladder.

In 1981, prior to my obtaining any computer training, my supervisor purchased four computers and told me to train the division on their usage. I successfully trained the division and then began automating various areas within the division. Soon after the training, I began taking computer classes which lead to my love of computers. Throughout my banking career I took various classes and workshops that were offered. Also from 1981 to 1983, I enrolled in a bank sponsored school called American Institute of Banking (A.I.B.), that provided me with 132 hours of training in accounting, data processing, business English, and psychology. Although I had taken several classes, I still had a desire to attend a formal institution and ultimately to receive my bachelor's degree. My daughter was growing, I was growing in my faith and I was growing in my job, but I still wanted a husband.

Ken and I met in August of 1986, through a mutual friend. Our relationship began as friends and we quickly realized that we had stronger feelings for one another. After four months, Ken proposed to me, and I accepted. We purchased a home prior to marriage, where Kisha and I lived until Ken and I were married in June of 1987. We honeymooned in Hawaii and three months later we found out that I was carrying twins. On March 12, 1988,

Elicia and Chaz were born. Kisha was nine when her siblings were born and was a big help to me taking care of twins.

I have since worked for several other organizations using the skills I acquired in my early years of education. In 2011, I graduated from Roberts Wesleyan College with a master of science in strategic leadership. I am now self-employed as a business consultant working with small and mid-size companies to meet their organizational needs. I am also a minister of the gospel of Jesus Christ. Kisha is living in Maryland and works as an HR manager. She grew up healthy, surrounded by family, and with a father who loves her .

I have changed from the time I had Kisha. I am older and wiser. I now know that commitment is more important than momentary, uncommitted, physical pleasure. I am thankful for the path that I took and for the gift Kisha is to me and our family. I survived the abuse of my father and overcame the potential to replicate his actions or to think like a victim. I accepted the hand that I was dealt, my father, and the cards that I chose, Larry and the decision to have premarital sex, and played them successfully to become the Christian, wife, mother, business owner, and now Grandmother of Aryanna & Derek, Jr. To God be the Glory.

[iii] http://www.ourbabynamer.com/meaning-of-Nakisha.html

Author's Corner

Biography: Rosa is a management consultant with over 20 years of diverse experiences in effective resource allocation. Her expertise centers on strategically conceptualizing, designing, building, and improving technical processes. Prior to her position as W.I.F.E (We Influence Future Excellence), Rosa was the operations manager for a non-profit, where she maintained on-site management of all business operations. Rosa has also worked as a miscellaneous information specialist (MIS) for a regional bank. Her responsibilities included identifying, eliminating, and/or relocating positions in order to meet cost reduction objectives while maintaining output integrity. Rosa received her B.A. in organizational management and M. S. in strategic leadership from Roberts Wesleyan College. Raised in Rochester, New York, Rosa and her husband Ken now live on three country acres in Ontario County. They are the proud parents of three adult children, Kisha, Elicia and Chaz, and grandparents of two beautiful grandchildren, Aryanna & Derek, Jr.. Rosa serves as a minister and on various leadership teams at Church of Love Faith Center in Rochester, NY.

Acknowledgments: To the one who changed my life: Jesus Christ, I shall forever be changed. To my husband, who has always loved, believed in and cherished me. You have taught me what a real man is. To my three children, having the three of you has been the best thing in my life. To my grandchildren: You two have taught me to play and love in a deeper way. To my brothers: Joseph, Nelson and Jeffery, you all are the best brothers a girl could ever ask for. To the sisters by another mother: Barbara T, Hollise, Gina, Glenda, Loretta, Nancy & Tracey, I love you all for who you are. To my other daughters: Leticia, Maya, Rosa and Dionne, you all are awesome women of God. To my brothers by another mother: Allan, Nate, Steve & Terry, I so appreciate you all in my life.

Contact Info:
Rosa Day
rday3@frontiernet.net
Facebook: https://www.facebook.com/rosa.day.12

THIRTEEN

LIFE AFTER BIRTH
Shiera Danice Goff

On Thursday, February 14, 1985, I died.

I was nineteen years old, twenty-one weeks pregnant and alone. Never would I have thought that things would go this way for me. I mean, statistically, I wasn't your typical teenage mother, but then again, I really was.

I was born in Rochester, New York and lived in Rochester until around the age of two when my mother sent me to live with my grandmother in Rubonia, Florida. I was too young to really know what was going on. The only thing that I knew was that I was surrounded by love. My grandmother was raising me along with four older male cousins. They watched over me and protected me. They were my family. I don't have any early memories of my mother.

To my family, I was Sherry Baby and I was spoiled. Life in Florida was good, but I didn't know any differently. My grandmother wasn't wealthy, but we were always well fed, clean and impeccably dressed.

I was five years old when I returned to live in Rochester. I don't remember leaving my grandmother. One day I was walking down the dirt roads of Rubonia, the next I was living in the 19th Ward in Rochester, New York, with my mother and father. I had a happy childhood. My mother worked for the county and my father was a student at the University of Rochester working towards a degree in accounting, eventually earning his CPA. I attended a private school and was an only child. Life was good.

I was eight, going on nine, when my first sister was born. By that time we were living in a townhome and my mother was completing her bachelor's degree in nursing from the University of Rochester. My father was working for a major accounting firm. We moved to the suburbs when I was ten and I couldn't have been happier. We lived in a four bedroom colonial style home with a huge yard and a neighborhood full of kids my age to play with.

My father got a job offer in Massachusetts and my happy existence was over. We had trouble selling our home that winter and my father had to leave us to begin his job in Boston while my pregnant mother stayed behind with my sister and me. My youngest sister was born when I was twelve and shortly after, my life changed dramatically.

We moved to a small suburban town an hour west of Boston. It was a huge culture shock for me, but things at home were different as well. My father had grown accustomed to living the single life for nearly a year and had a difficult time readjusting to family life. At that time, I also began to question my paternity.

I confided in a relative that I wasn't certain that the man I had been calling daddy was actually my father. I was too young and naïve to understand the word *biological*. I just knew that things didn't add up and sadly my suspicions were right. When I was thirteen years old, I received a phone call from a man claiming to actually *be* my biological father. He told me that I was his first born child and claimed that he had stayed away because he was following my mother's wishes. From there, my life became hell. My mother found out that I was communicating with my biological father, my Massachusetts father began philandering on a regular basis and life in our cozy New England home was increasingly volatile.

I had become angry, resentful and bitter towards my parents. The secret she had hidden for years had finally come to light and my mother, not knowing how to handle the situation, forbade me to contact my biological father and took her anger out on me. I became more and more depressed. I was unhappy at home and my only escape was school and getting involved in any and every extra-curricular activity so I could stay away from home. When I didn't have a choice but to be in the house, I stayed in my room most of the time. My grades suffered; I had failed that school year and had basically given up. My grandmother asked my mother to send me back to her.

At the age of seventeen, I was again living with my grandmother in Rubonia, Florida. Things had changed slightly, but much still remained the same. The roosters still crowed in the morning, my 'Annie' was still operating her general store, but Mr. Webb, the white man that owned the grocery store and ran the post office, had passed. Some of the dirt roads had been paved over and my grandmother had more modern amenities like a microwave and a dishwasher. I had also changed and my grandmother had a hard time adjusting to a teenage 'Sherry' versus the five year old one who last lived under her roof. Although I had spent many summer vacations with my grandmother, she was now my primary guardian and was very strict. I was not allowed to *run the streets*. I had to be home after band practice and Friday night football games. I was not allowed to *take company*. Although she had a firm hand, I was much happier in her home than I ever was in Massachusetts.

I had finished school and was eighteen years old. My mother wanted me to return to Massachusetts, but that was the last place I wanted to be. I decided to visit my father in Rochester. Now that I was eighteen and out of her house, my mother couldn't stop me from seeing him. That's where my life took another sharp turn. In Rochester, I met several half siblings that I had only read about in letters and met the sister that was very close to my age. She convinced me to stay for the summer and I got a job as a camp counselor.

That summer trouble entered wearing a black Speedo.

He was five years older than me. I was eighteen; he was twenty three, a Marine and a junior at the University of Rochester studying computer science. He worked at the camp as a water safety instructor. To me, he was beautiful. He was 6' 3", extremely muscular, athletic, and had the deepest, darkest chocolate skin that I had ever seen on a man.

Although I had experienced a lot in my short life, I had never met anyone like him and wasn't prepared for the games that he was about to play with me emotionally. What I didn't learn until later was that I was only supposed to be his summer fling while his girlfriend was away for the summer. Another discovery was that she happened to live directly across the street from me. I'm sure he was looking over his shoulder each time he visited me at home, hoping that her roommates who stayed in town for the summer didn't spot him.

I was intimidated by him. I mean, he was older, in college, more worldly and experienced. We dated casually. He took me on a few dates, invited me to frat parties, but he was mostly interested in getting into my pants.

One August morning I woke to extremely sharp abdominal pains. I was back in Massachusetts visiting my family and alone in the house. The pain hurt so badly I could barely walk and literally crawled to the bathroom from my bedroom. I pulled the bathroom rugs away so I could feel the cold of the ceramic tile against my skin. I was sweating and suddenly began dry heaving into the toilet. I was scared, but didn't want to call my mother at work because deep down I knew what was wrong. I stayed there on the bathroom floor for what seemed like an eternity.

Once I felt okay, I grabbed the yellow pages and searched for a clinic. I found one not too far away, called, made an appointment, rode my bike to the clinic and several hours later received the news. I was pregnant.

I shared this news first with the father of my child. He said that he would support me 110 percent with whatever I decided to do, but when I announced that I was keeping the baby, he wasn't as supportive as he originally offered and that percentage rate dropped to about three.

My biological father was disappointed, but supportive. He told me that I had to tell my parents myself and put me on a plane. My father picked me up at the airport and during that hour-long drive from Logan Airport to our home he shared with me how he was worried for me and didn't want me to become a statistic. I sat there listening and wishing he had opened up to me like this long before. My mother came to my room that evening, sat on the side of my bed with a glass of wine and opened up to me about her hopes and dreams for her first born daughter. She thought I was going to be Miss America and because I was always so interested in writing, a famous author. In her eyes, everything that she dreamed for her daughter was now gone. My mother was also embarrassed. Although those words never came out of her mouth, I was her eighteen year old daughter, carrying an illegitimate child.

Just about everyone I spoke to had advice for me.

"You're not ready to raise a child", or, "A child will slow you down", or, "There are adoption agencies that can help you find a loving home for your baby", (*like my home wouldn't be as loving*), and the worst of all, "You should have an abortion."

The baby I was carrying was now my responsibility. I made the decision to have unprotected sex and I had to accept responsibility for my actions.

I returned to Rochester and found a part time job working in a shoe store. I hid my pregnancy from my boss. My first trimester had been going smoothly, but my hormones were off the charts! I cried often, usually over the father of my unborn child. I only had had the one bout of morning sickness and later caught a cold that turned into walking pneumonia because I was too afraid to take any cold medicines for fear that it would hurt my baby.

And then I died.

I had just finished grocery shopping and had carried the bags up two flights of stairs. After putting the food away, went into my room to lie down. I kept feeling a cramping sensation and after consulting a few people, called my doctor. My doctor suggested I see him right away and during my examination told me that I was in labor and was three centimeters dilated. He sent me directly to the hospital.

I was given a medication to stop or slow my contractions and was advised that this treatment might lower my blood pressure. A nurse checked my blood pressure every fifteen minutes. I lay there in a large, white, sterile room alone, listening to the thumping of my baby's heartbeat on the fetal monitor and an occasional whoosh as it wiggled around in my uterus.

I was cold.

The nurse entered again and checked my pressure.

"Shiera, how do you feel?" She asked.

"I'm okay," I answered. "I'm cold. I'm tired."

"I'll get you some more blankets. Don't go to sleep, okay? Shiera, don't go to sleep."

The whooshing noise and beating of my baby's heart on the fetal monitor suddenly changed to the ringing of emergency call bells. Out of nowhere, doctors and nurses rushed into the room and began to frantically work on me. No one said anything to me. No one was talking to me. I didn't know what was going on, but I was amazingly calm as I looked on. I wasn't watching from the hospital bed though. I was looking at them from another corner of the room.

I looked on as the hospital staff worked feverishly to revive me and save my life and that of my unborn child. I had coded. I really don't know what happened but I have said for years that God watches over the babies and the fools and that evening, He watched over my baby and me. I wasn't looking on from the corner anymore.

Suddenly I was back in my bed and a doctor was talking to me, "Shiera, we're going to send you to Strong Memorial Hospital where they have the facilities to handle high risk pregnancies like yours."

They packed me up, put me in an ambulance and sent me off to the High Risk Unit. Once I arrived, nurses got me situated in the room that would be mine for the next three weeks.

Once settled, I remember a staff doctor greeting me with, "I hear you gave them quite a scare over at Highland!"

At about twenty four weeks, I was discharged and released to the care of an aunt with strict orders to remain on bed rest. My mother had not visited.

I returned to the High Risk Unit for two more stays and in between each visit went back to stay with my aunt. During that time, she hosted a baby shower for me. My mother did not come.

On the morning of Thursday, March 28, 1985, I remember lying in bed listening to my cousin's radio playing softly in the other room. Madonna's *Crazy for You* was on the air. I lay there feeling as if I needed to use the bathroom. I convinced myself to get up and as soon as I did, liquid spilled all over the linoleum floor. I lifted my nightgown and stood there legs spread apart, comprehending what had just happened.

At 8:59 a.m. I gave birth to a baby boy and sobbed when they announced his sex and heard his first cries. He was the most beautiful baby that I had ever seen. The nurses called him a little peanut. He was five weeks early and weighed in at five pounds, four ounces. Delivered by cesarean, his skin was perfect; no wrinkles, no flakes and he had a head full of jet black hair that lay flat on his head like a little Indian baby. When they were open, he had the biggest, widest, darkest eyes; like black marbles.

I named him Christopher.

When I was able to walk on my own I went to the nursery late one night and was heartbroken to discover that he had been separated from the other babies and put in an isolette. A nurse helped him out of the isolette and handed him to me. My baby boy and I sat in a dark little corner of the nursery all by ourselves, just the two of us. I rocked back and forth in the rocking chair and sang *Precious Lord, Take My Hand* to my little boy. It was just me and him against the world.

The day that Christopher and I were released, I remember how all of the nurses and staff happily waved goodbye to me. I had gotten to know a lot of them very well, since Strong had been my home for a couple of months. As I was wheeled out the front door of the hospital with my baby boy in my arms, I remember becoming very concerned and thought to myself, "Wait, the baby is coming *with* me?"

Even after a near death experience, three hospital stays totaling five weeks, an emergency C-section and a week-long recovery, my mother had still not come to see me. The first time she actually saw Christopher was when he was four months old and I drove to Massachusetts.

I moved back to Massachusetts and lived there until Christopher was eleven months old. I had reunited with my high school sweetheart, but that relationship had become emotionally abusive and had the potential to become physically abusive. Naturally, things weren't going well between my mother and me and when she had the first opportunity to get me back to Rochester, she did. *That* was her first visit back to Rochester.

Upon my arrival to Rochester, I found a shelter for young mothers and stayed there for about a month. Christopher and I shared a tiny room on the first floor of a house that used to be the rectory for the Catholic Church next door. They helped get me on my feet as well as find housing. It was a depressing time for me. Luckily, my baby was too young to know what was going on. While at the shelter, I learned that I was pregnant again. The father was the emotionally abusive ex-boyfriend in Massachusetts and I knew that by having his child, I would be forever tied to him. I couldn't do it. I searched out a doctor and scheduled an abortion. The day of the procedure, I rode the bus by myself to the hospital. I filled out the forms, went into the room and ended my pregnancy, crying the entire time and alone once again. I rode the bus back to the shelter and recovered in my tiny room, never telling a soul, until now.

Not knowing much about neighborhoods in Rochester, I rented an apartment on the City's northeast side. It wasn't the greatest area, but I had my own place. It was a studio apartment with French doors separating the living room from the bedroom. When I moved in, all I had was a love seat, a dinette table that someone gave me, two kitchen chairs, Christopher's high chair, a mattress on the bedroom floor and Christopher's crib, tucked in the corner of the bedroom.

That year I registered and became a student at Monroe

Community College, majoring in Communications and Media Arts. People told me that having a child would slow me down, but I was determined to prove them wrong. I found the perfect daycare for Christopher and while his mommy was starting school, so was he. He was eighteen months old and I was so worried for him because he had only been with me and other family members. His first morning at day care, Christopher ran off to play with the other kids and forgot about his mommy. I was heartbroken and his teacher saw my pain. "Honey, let me tell you something," his teacher said. "To a little boy, his mother will always be his first love."

She assured me that he would come running into my arms at the end of the day and sure enough, she was right except my little man wrapped his arms around my legs when he saw me that afternoon.

A chance interview led me to a job at a local radio station. I was so excited because communications was my major and this might be a foot in the door. I was mostly doing data entry work, calling record companies and organizing the music library, but it was a start. My first semester went well and I was excited to be in college. Unfortunately, I allowed too many obstacles and distractions to get in my way. I didn't finish out the school year.

I continued to work at the radio station and after an attempted sexual assault in my apartment, moved out of that neighborhood. Over the next year or two, I worked odd jobs and enrolled at MCC again. During my second semester there, I met the man who would eventually become my husband. He appeared to be different from most guys that I had been involved with. He came off as soft spoken, kind and compassionate. He was safe. And Christopher liked him. We married two years later.

As we approached our second year of marriage, things weren't going well and I thought about leaving my husband until I found out that I was pregnant again. He and I had one unsuccessful pregnancy and as with my pregnancy with Christopher, I went into premature labor about the middle of my sixth month. I worked as a bank teller, standing on my feet for eight hours a day and walked to and from work. I was put on bed rest and eventually landed in the hospital for four weeks. I was released and assigned a home health aide, but was admitted to the hospital for another two weeks. I was able to successfully carry to full term, but had an emergency cesarean and delivered a seven pound, fifteen ounce baby boy. My mother did not visit.

After an extended maternity leave, I went back to work at the bank. On the day of my baby's first birthday, I was robbed. The robber handed me a note reading, "It's not your money, so why die?" and I wholeheartedly agreed and handed him the money. I realized that I was not meant to be a bank teller for the rest of my life. I didn't want to look back at my life on my death bed and have any regrets and knew that getting my degree would lead to a better life, not just for me, but for my family as well. My husband once told me that I never finished what I started and those words gave me more than enough motivation to prove to myself, to him and to my mother that I could and *would* succeed. Earning my degree was make or break for me. I had allowed so many distractions and obstacles to slow me down in the past and it wasn't going to happen again.

I finished my requirements at MCC in record time and

transferred to the State University of New York at Brockport. Marital problems prevented me from finishing on time. He was supportive in the beginning, but not so much so as I got closer to the finish line. I graduated and walked across the stage a year later with my Bachelors of Science degree in communications and broadcasting.

Not long after graduating, my marriage ended. From the beginning, it wasn't a good marriage and if I could go back in time to change anything in my life it would be that. We came from two different worlds.

Because I had a family, landing a job in my field was difficult. Since I wasn't able to relocate to other cities, it took a few years to get my foot in the door and once I did, I kicked it wide open. I was hired as a morning radio show co-host for an R&B/Hip-Hop radio station. While there, our show had the highest ratings in the station's history. I had the opportunity to interview dozens of celebrities, athletes, entertainers and politicians. That job led me to getting hired as a news reporter for an ABC News affiliate in Rochester. My dream to be a news reporter had been fulfilled, but I learned that I was cut from a different cloth from some of the people in that business. It's an 'every man/woman for themselves' mentality and that's not who I was then or now. I worked there for two years before being hired in my current position.

I love what I do. My job has opened so many doors for me and established me as a recognizable and respected name in the community. It has also given me financial stability and freedom for the first time in my adult life. I haven't forgotten where I came from and pay it forward by hiring interns to get hands on experience and a head start. Growing up, I didn't have anyone that I could really turn to when I was going through hard times and I take the time to mentor young women whenever I can.

I am in a good place now. It took me a long time to get here. God did something to me. He opened my eyes and showed me my blessings. God has given me a second chance at life and it took a while for me to realize that. He has blessed me in so many ways. I purchased my own home five years ago; I have traveled to the Caribbean, taken cruises and fulfilled my lifelong dream of going to Paris.

Interestingly enough, my mother recently told me how proud of me she is. She understands that I did not take the traditional route to get to where I am today. She knows that I had to overcome a lot and I am happy that she recognizes that. Our relationship is still strained. I want for her to understand how I felt when she wasn't there for me. I want her to recognize that her daughter needed her when she was alone in the hospital and scared.

Christopher and I have had our ups and downs over the years. We battled often when he was a teenager and there were a few times when I thought that he might cause me to have an aneurism from yelling at him. He's a grown man now and the father of a handsome and precocious two year old that carries his name. I pray for my son often. He, too, is taking the long route to get to wherever it is that he is trying to go. I just hope he has it mapped out on his GPS. He and his fiancée are expecting their second child, a girl. Her parents have honored me by giving her my middle name. I pray that her life will be less complicated and that she will conquer the world. Like I said,

God watches over the babies and the fools and I know that He gave me Christopher for a reason. I tried to raise him the best that I could. I know that I made a few mistakes along the way. Sometimes I wish that I was older, more mature and settled when he came into my life.

Christopher was my blessing. I can't even imagine what my life would be like had God not chosen me to be his mommy. He knows that he is my first born child and holds a special place in my heart. He calls me his hero and honors me not only on Mother's Day, but on Father's Day, as well.

I've come a long way since the day that I died and I still have a long way to go. I was asked if I considered my life a success and my answer was no. There is so much more that I want to accomplish, so much more that I want to do.

I'll know when I get there.

Author's Corner

Biography: Shiera Danice Goff was born in Rochester, New York, but lived in Rubonia, Florida, Holliston, Massachusetts and Rochester during her childhood. Although she has been in Rochester for most of her adult life, she considers herself a Florida girl at heart. They say that home is where the heart is and her heart belongs in Rubonia, Florida with her grandmother. Shiera currently works for the Mayor of Rochester in the Bureau of Communications where she is the Communications Producer. She earned her bachelor's of science degree in broadcast communications from the State University of New York at Brockport . Her career took off in 2001 when she was hired to co-host the morning show at an R&B and Hip-Hop radio station. While there, the morning show had its highest ratings in the station's history. Shiera has met and interviewed dozens of recording artists, actors, athletes and politicians. In 2004 she began working as a news reporter for an ABC News affiliate in Rochester where she found her niche as a human interest reporter. Former Mayor, Robert Duffy, hired Shiera to work under his administration in 2006. Shiera currently produces and hosts a community affairs talk show for the City of Rochester. She produces and voices television and radio commercials, public service announcements and provides video production services for city departments. She is a 2007 graduate of the African American Leadership Development Program (AALDP), a member of the National Association of Black Journalists, and The City of Rochester's Black Heritage Committee. She has participated in several mentoring programs for young women and has sat on committees for Big Brothers/Big Sisters of Greater Rochester and the Boy Scouts of America. She is a member of Mount Olivet Baptist Church and serves on the

Usher Board Ministry. Never forgetting where she came from and how she got to where she is, Shiera pays it forward by hiring interns to learn and get hands on experience in the broadcasting field. In 2009, Shiera was profiled as a Woman to Watch by *HerRochester* Magazine. She is a contributing writer/food blogger for the *Democrat and Chronicle* newspaper and having been recently diagnosed with Celiac Disease, writes about her daily struggles with finding enjoyable gluten free foods.

Acknowledgments:
I've come this far by faith. I know that through it all, God was watching over me. He may not have been happy with every decision that I made and I'm sure there were times when I could feel Him reaching down to knock some sense into me! I want to thank my children for giving me strength. Much of what I do and what I have accomplished is because of them. To Christopher, it's wonderful to be your mommy.

Contact Info:
Shiera Danice Goff
mizzgoff@gmail.com
Facebook: https://www.facebook.com/shiera.coleman

The Voice of
The *Adult* Child

Bonus Section

*Your children are the greatest gift God will give to you, and their souls the
heaviest responsibility He will place in your hands. Take time with them,
teach them to have faith in God. Be a person in whom they can have faith.
When you are old, nothing else you've done will have mattered as much.*
Lisa Wingate

THE BIRTHDAY BLUES
Tiffiney Taylor

Although my mother and father have forsaken me, yet the Lord will take me up. (Psalms 27:10 AMP)

For the first time in my life, I knew what it felt like to experience pain. The kind of pain that is inflicted on you by somebody else as a result of his or her own selfish behavior. That day, it felt as if my heart were being ripped from my chest and my soul were being snatched from the core of my being. It just didn't seem real that something this disturbing was happening to me. I remember this day like it was yesterday, so fresh and vivid is it in my mind.

It was the spring of 1980 and I was 7 years old. It was supposed to be a happy day in my life, but it became, one of the worst days of my life. A day I have never forgotten. My aunt had planned a birthday party for me at one of the hottest spots in town, McDonald's. Somebody else had alternative plans, secret plans that no one else knew. As we were preparing to leave for the party, no one could anticipate what was about to happen. Suddenly, I was being forced to leave the comforts of my home and the people I knew best, to go with a woman I barely even knew. You see this woman was my mother. She wasn't actively involved in my life but she was determined to force me to go with her. When I refused, all chaos broke loose. I wonder what made her think that she had a right to come and disrupt my life? I could still hear the sounds of my screams.

"No! No! No! I don't want to go with you, I don't even know you," I yelled, my face soaked with tears. My little heart was frightened, but deep down inside I knew I had to fight. I was determined to stay right where I was in the place I called home.

I positioned myself on the bottom step gripping tight to the wood banister adjacent to the front door.

I could feel her pulling on me shouting. "You are my daughter and you are coming with me!"

All I could do was cry harder and hold tighter while looking to my grandmother for help. I could hear my grandmother pleading with my mother to leave me alone and go on about her business. But she was just as determined as I and we fought against each other. The harder she pulled the stronger I held on. Once she figured out that I wasn't going to let go, she began to loosen her grip on my arm.

Finally, the police arrived. I'm not sure who called them and it didn't even matter. I began to feel a sigh of relief thinking they would be on my side, but I was wrong. I stood there listening to everyone tell her side of the story, shouting and screaming trying to make her voice heard. With my feet firmly planted and my little arms still wrapped around the banister, I looked the police officer straight in the eye. My voice trembled.

"I don't want to go!" I pleaded.

But the officer told me I had to go because my grandmother had no legal documentation stating I was in her care and custody. My heart dropped. That was not what I wanted to hear. I couldn't believe I was being forced to leave with a woman I barely knew just because she was my biological mother. I pleaded with the police not to make me go but they said I had no choice. Believe me, I went kicking and screaming out the front door, down the cement steps, and into a burgundy BMW parked in front of the house.

My screams became louder and stronger. My tears fell faster as I yelled for my grandma to save me. Before I was shoved in the backseat of the car, my eyes met my grandmother's. She stood there helpless. I can still hear the sound of the car door slamming shut. As the car sped away, I remember beating on the window yelling for help. All I wanted was to be free. I was crying so intensely that my nose began to bleed. I guess you could imagine, I was emotionally, mentally, and physically drained, but I was determined to not give up.

As the night drew near and all the ruckus of the day had ceased, I was planning my way of escape. I'm sure my mother had to be exhausted from the events of the day. She fell soundly asleep because she used alcohol as a way of numbing herself. Once I knew she was sleeping, I packed some clothes in a brown paper bag and left. I did it. I escaped into a dark and cold night and began my journey back to 1035 Genesee Street. Don't ask me how I did it, but I made my way home walking from the Northwest side of the city to the Southwest side. Finally, I arrived safely on the porch and knocked on the door. This was the end to my new beginning.

I had been living with my maternal grandmother since I was about 2 years old. She never legally adopted me because she didn't want to go through the hassle of the court system or of fighting with my mother. By now she had already experienced enough heartache. She had raised eight children of her own and then supported a daughter who became pregnant at 15 and gave birth at 16. She did the next best thing for me and took on the responsibility of raising me when my parents proved they were incapable or unwilling. My father was 19 years old at the time and he had hopes of attending college on a basketball scholarship but those dreams shattered when I was born. They weren't bad parents, I suppose, just not mature enough to handle the responsibility of caring for a child. I give them credit though. They tried to make it work. Heck, my grandmother even signed the paperwork authorizing my mother to get married, but her's was not a marriage made in heaven. When my parents separated, my mother lived life on her own terms. Eventually, my father moved to the West Coast, creating a new life for himself, one that would not include me. I became the sole responsibility of my maternal grandmother.

Even though I had the love and support of my grandmothers (maternal/paternal), aunts, and uncles, I always felt like there was a void in my life. I still felt abandoned and unloved. *"Why don't my parents want me?"* I always asked myself. I never really felt as if I were a part of a cohesive family unit. There were times when I did not feel included in family functions. For instance, one day my family was gathered in the kitchen having a jolly good time and I felt as if I were being disregarded. I'm sure it was nothing intentional but I was craving attention and my feelings were hurt. So I decided to do something about it. I marched my little self up stairs and automatically, in a rage of anger, began to destroy my grandmother's bedroom. I pulled clothes out the drawers, wiped things off the dresser, and threw things across the room.

When asked why I did this I huffed, "Because nobody loves me."

One would think this was headline news the way they responded. Immediately, my family reassured me that I was indeed loved. Still, the love of my mother and father was missing. And I had to clean up the mess I made! My grandmother made that very clear.

I would see my mother periodically, but there was no emotional connection or love felt. Meanwhile, my dad was on the other side of the country and had started a new life, with a new family. There were no happy birthdays, Christmas presents, or routine phone calls to see how I was doing in school. Well, none that I can remember. Heck, there wasn't even financial support to help my grandmother provide for me. It took a village to raise me with my grandma as the leader. Thank God for my grandmothers, grandfather, aunts, and uncles who stepped up to the plate to make sure I was the most loved little girl in the world. Although they couldn't take the place of my parents, they sure did a great job!

For most of my childhood, I struggled with low self-esteem and insecurities. I never knew exactly how I fit in. I often questioned whether or not I was accepted by anyone. I became reclusive and held my feelings inside. It was like I became numb to the pain inside me. It was difficult to build relationships because I always feared I would be hurt. There were times when I felt inadequate, not good enough, and I often found myself overcompensating as I tried to fill the void left by my parents. I didn't understand who I was. Who was this girl named Tiffiney? Why did my parents give me up so easily? Wasn't I good enough for them?

My mother made several attempts to strengthen our relationship, but it was always shrouded with controversy and awkwardness. Remember, this woman was not actively involved in my life and I had no emotional connection to her. As I was talking on the phone with my friend, a daily routine for me after school, my mother came by for an unexpected visit and immediately started barking orders at me. My immediate response?

"You are not my mother and you can't tell me what to do."

As the tension began to rise, I felt like I was being attacked by a stranger and I immediately went into a defensive mode. As things escalated, it went from a shouting match to a fight. To protect myself, I began to hit her repeatedly with the phone until my grandfather separated us. I'm sure this was a result of bottled up anger. By no means am I proud of this, but this was our reality as mother and daughter. Nothing could have prepared me for these experiences, but they would become the story of my life, shaping me as a young girl who would eventually become a woman. I don't think my life ever became "normal." I just learned to live with the cards I was dealt. There was nothing that could ever fill that void.

I often imagined how different my life would be if I were being raised by one or both of my parents. I wished that we had positive and healthy relationships And that they would become a part of my life, cheering me on at sporting events, listening to me sing in the choir, watching me get ready for the prom, and being that shoulder to cry on. Would they be there to watch me graduate from high school, or be there to give me away on my wedding day? I must say my mother was present for some of the major milestones in my life but my father was not. I don't think he ever made any real attempt to be. I think I wanted a relationship with my father more than anything. I wanted to be a daddy's girl. Maybe it was because he lived so far away and I didn't have much contact with him.

I thought for sure he would want to be present for the biggest day of my life, but he didn't. I remember the day I received that dreaded phone call. My feelings towards my father would never be the same. My grandmother called me at work and broke the news to me.

"Your father will not be giving you away on your wedding day. He will not even be attending the wedding."

Without any explanation, he was not going to be there to see his little girl on her special day. All I can remember was that I sobbed uncontrollably for hours, maybe even days. I just knew for sure this would be a day he would not want to miss, but I was wrong. What could have possibly prevented him from coming? As a little girl, all I ever wanted was my daddy. I wanted us to build happy memories together. But I never got that opportunity. Tell me how do you heal a broken heart?

Today, I stand tall on the shoulders of those who have gone before me. It is by God's grace that I have been able to work hard and become the best woman I could be. Growing up, I always imagined how my life would end up. I always knew I wanted to make something of myself and to not be a victim of my circumstances. I wanted to make my family and myself proud. With my morals and values in hand, I headed off to St. John Fisher College as the first generation in my family to attend college. I worked part-time jobs to support myself through school. I gave birth to my son during my junior year and I did not allow that to deter my success. I stayed the course, completed my studies, and graduated with a bachelor's of arts. Eventually, I married and expanded my family all while obtaining and pursuing degrees in higher education, working in ministry, and building a successful career.

My greatest accomplishments to date are being a loving, devoted wife and mother. I'm grateful to God that I have been able to provide my children with tangible things in life such as, morals, values, love, a stable two-parent home, a good education, and my being present in all areas of their lives. I can say that I'm a proud mother. I'm honored to say that I have healthy, positive relationships with my sons. We have built wonderful, lifetime memories; something I didn't have as a child with my parents. Not only have I been able to do this for my children, but I have also paid it forward by raising my youngest sister.

I'm happy to say that I have an amiable relationship with my mother. We appreciate and support each other. Our relationship is still a work in progress, but we are willing make it healthier. I know that if I need her she will be there for me and my family. I will admit, it hasn't always been easy, but it has been worth it. When I think about my story, it's inconceivable to think that I'm a survivor!

Author's Corner

Biography: Tiffiney Taylor, a native Rochesterian and graduate of Our Lady of Mercy High School, acquired a bachelor of arts in gerontology from St. John Fisher College with a minor in religious studies and a concentration in sociology. She also received a masters of social work from Roberts Wesleyan College. Tiffiney is currently pursuing a master of divinity from Northeastern Seminary. Tiffiney has had the opportunity to work in the human service field for over 15 years. Tiffiney currently works as a social worker for Rochester General Health Systems. Committed to serving her community, Tiffiney serves on several boards and committees. A licensed evangelist, Tiffiney loves sharing the word of the Lord. In 2009, Tiffiney began pursuing her passion as a lifestyle coach. She became the President and CEO of Breathe Anew. Breathe Anew is a firm offering a variety of personal and professional coaching services. Specially practiced and educated, she coaches women, men and children; assisting them in recognizing their potential and taping into their greatness. Her goal is to help people develop passion and vision with a desire to live in their existence and divine purpose. Tiffiney is a lifestyle coach who inspires, encourages and transforms lives! Most importantly, she will support you in liberating your mind, body and spirit to live a life full of potential.

Acknowledgments: I am grateful to God for trusting me with such a wonderful opportunity. I dedicate this JTM project to my grandparents, Dave, Louetta, and Margret. Words cannot explain how appreciative I am for you filling a missing void in my life. I will always love you. To my husband, Alan, thanks for believing in and supporting my dreams. I love you! My son's: Jalen, DeVin, and Alan, Jr., you are exceptional young men and I love you. To my parents, Jeff and Judy, I'm glad God chose you to bring life to my soul. To my village of family who were influential in my upbringing, I salute you, especially my Aunties. To my sisters, Chassity and Aaliyah, we are survivors! Much love! To Tamara and Whitney, I love you. To my sista girls, thanks for always holding it down (you know who you are). To Pastor Green, thanks for your spiritual leadership. Thanks to all my family, friends, and supporters. To this powerful team of extraordinary women, the JTM Authors, thank you ladies for taking this journey with me. Thank you, LaShunda; words cannot explain how grateful I am for your vision and your belief that my story was as equally important. Continue to follow the path God has set before you.

Contact Info:
Tiffiney Carter Taylor
PO Box 64185
Rochester, NY 14624
www.breatheanew.com
tbreathe@gmail.com
Facebook: https://www.facebook.com/tiffineytaylor
Twitter: @tiffineytaylor
Phone: 585.802.6895
Fax: 585.270.8399

BONUS

NO THORNS IN MY GARDEN
Rafael Johnson

Ralphy, TJ, Monica, Stephen, Keisha, Shandola, and Grandma comprised the household in which I lived in from age three to seven. My mother gave birth to me at quite a young age. She was sixteen, still in high school, still maturing as a person—a woman, rather, still learning the ropes of life herself. As she finished high school and went onto college at SUNY Brockport, I lived in Utica, NY, with my grandmother. Though she was a couple of hours away, my mother still visited on the weekends whenever possible and she never missed an important event in my life, especially birthdays and holidays.

I can't help but find it difficult to remember my father. He was much of an in and out kind of person, or at least that was the only impression he had left me with. Not to say he wasn't a good person in general, but more so a person I had not fully learned about.

I can remember him picking me up a few times to see my brothers. Sadly, I cannot remember their names nor remember how many in total there are anymore. But I can certainly recall the fun we had as kids. Roaring laughter and running footsteps echo deep inside my mind. Those are the only things that proved that the memories of my brothers weren't dreams. Those thoughts are reminders that they were all real and we were once all together. I was young, but I remember my mom being there whenever I needed her, calling often, holding me, telling me we were going to move soon and that she was working on our life together. I couldn't wait. I still longed for the relationship with my father.

When I finished second grade, my mother found an apartment in Rochester, NY, which became my new home. When my mother met my stepfather, Cory Johnson, I was very young and our relationship, at first, was a bit bumpy. I was still stuck on my biological father and wasn't exactly allowing Cory to get any closer. I know now he was trying his best to develop a relationship with me. But I was young, and to me, my father was my father and no one was going to take his place. As I think about it now, I honestly feel a hint of stupidity defending someone who left.

Over time, Cory and I became much closer and the memory of my father started to hide in the shadows of my subconscious mind and I was sure to keep it that way. Dad, (Cory), married my mother, and I became an older brother. Mom gave birth to many more siblings. But no matter how big our family grew, something was still missing. I still felt a bit out of place or constantly felt as though I didn't belong. I was still Rafael Wendell Walker.

I didn't feel like a Rafael Wendell Walker just, Rafael. Your name should be something you cherish and I certainly did not cherish mine. I shared a name with someone that was, to me, a bad example of a father. Why was I carrying this curse?

The discussion of adoption was without question something I had been waiting for. I had felt like a Johnson much of my life so the choice was left in my hands. Did I want to officially be known as Rafael Wendell Johnson? Or did I want to still be known as Rafael Wendell Walker?

That question was much easier to answer than any other. It should not have even been a question, just simply a ready, set, go! Once the adoption was finalized, I received my new birth certificate. My biological father's name was no longer there. The name I was born with, Rafael Wendell Walker was no longer there either. Instead, Rafael Wendell Johnson was now in my name place and Cory Johnson was now placed as my father. I no longer felt out of place. I had no more questions about where I came from or where Rafael Mercado Walker was. No more questions about my being the only Walker in the household and this, Cory Johnson, was my father.

Dad has been there for me since day one. We have come a long way and I learned we shared so many things in common. I am more like him than Ralph. Blood would not make us closer, nor would blood convince me that I don't come from Cory Johnson.

I even tell people that today when asked, "Is he your father?"

I answer, "Yes, he is my father. I come from him."

When I think of my mother, she fought for everything she needed, as I grew up watching. I knew she would never lose a battle. Most people find it hard to be motivated and have high expectations of themselves. But for her, it was second nature. She had inherited the gifts of devotion and self-discipline which became the cornerstones to her success, not only as a woman, but as an educated African-American woman. There is certainly a difference.

She has achieved her bachelor's degree in education, and has even achieved her master's of education. Now, she has planned to go on yet another educational journey to earn her doctorate degree.

Seeing what I have seen her achieve, and knowing what I know she can do, my mother will have that doctorate degree and soon. She is the reason I found my own methods of self-motivation. She is the reason I think heavily about my future and do not limit myself to the bare minimums of life. She is the reason why I am able to recognize my full potential and have the faith and confidence it takes to be a successful man and human being. She gave me life and there is not a life I can live for her that does the justice of saying thank you. But I can do my best to show her appreciation by being all that I can be.

There was a time when I had many questions that I felt needed answers. Questions about my biological father. Questions that I'm sure most kids with an absentee parent asked growing up. What did I do to make him leave? Was I not good enough? Did he not want me? Did he not care? Did he love me?

The last memory I can remember of my father was on April 23, 1995. I asked him if I would see him the next day for my birthday. He said he would come and I really had hope that he was going to be there. He wasn't. My mother never said anything negative about him and always made it a point to say that he was not able to father me because of his own issues that had nothing to do with me. Those excuses worked for a while but as I got older, I grew more upset by his absence. Although I know mom didn't want me to feel pain, I still felt the pain of a boy trying to understand why he was unwanted by his biological father. Through the years, I had not received a birthday card nor a letter in the mail. No visits or phone calls. Even though my stepfather –father in my own words — was around, my biological father still had a piece of me that always saddened me. It was the memory that apart from brothers, he too, was real. He was in my life before, he did hold me, and he was there in the beginning. But that changed and he is not here now.

I sometimes wonder where I would be if he had not left. Would my mother and I be with him? A family? Would I be in a better position than where I stand now or the opposite? Would we be happy? Eventually, those questions of curiosity turned into not caring at all. But who can you blame?

While I was attending Morgan State University, he finally reached out. Raw emotions like anger, sadness, and frustration overwhelmed me. His message, his hello, was almost 14 years too late. I messaged how I felt and I certainly did not plan on letting him off easy. The contents of his reply weren't exactly what I expected and it seemed as though he were making excuses. It took a lot of time, after receiving a number of messages from him for me to reply back. We took things slow, but over time, I drifted away from him.

Today, we don't talk and we both know how to find each other. He is in the position of waiting for me now, but I'm in the position of looking away from him. If I wanted to, if I really wanted to, I could find him. I'm just not going to at this moment in my life.

It is because of two great parents that I was awarded and received great recognition, particularly in elementary school. I was awarded the Do The Right Thing Award every other month, if not every month. I was awarded Star Reader, What Would Jesus Do, and Student of the Year awards. And before graduating from St. Monica's elementary school, I was awarded a five-year, $50,000 academic Xavier Scholarship to attend McQuaid Jesuit High School. I finished my last year of high school at Bishop Kearney. I received my diploma, and in the fall, I was off on a new journey to Baltimore, Maryland to attend Morgan State University.

My time at Morgan State, majoring in theater arts, lasted one year. It was not because I was asked to leave the college due to any delinquencies or poor academic performance. No. Leaving was my decision—one I spent much of my time thinking about. The teachers were great, my friends were amazing, the parties were every day, and the food was very satisfying. What more could a college student possibly ask for in a university?

My struggle was completely internal. I had discovered many things about myself that were utterly surprising. I was trying new things that I told myself I would never do. I became distant from my family and my girlfriend at the time. My means of comfort came from the attention of girls and partying, not checking in with anyone at home and ignoring calls. Whenever I was going through a tough time, I found myself angry at God and soon, I started to completely drift away from my faith and questioned if there was a God at all.

I knew I was changing, but I was changing faster than I was able to keep up. I tried to hide my emotions by keeping myself busy with having fun and soon started slacking on my school work. I was never the best student, but I also had no excuse to fail. I began to dig deep within, as I came from a home that was rooted in faith in God. I looked back on all the times I felt weak, alone, or confused and remembered feeling the presence of God through all those moments. Faith became what motivated me to do more than what I was doing.

In April, second semester, I had convinced myself that I was not only changing, but I was very homesick. I was weak. I could not bear being away and I was afraid I would wake up and never be myself again. I called my family, tears flowing down my face, not knowing if they would let me leave a college to come home because I couldn't stick it out. But they did. They told me if it was something I was completely sure of doing, then they would bring me home at the end of the semester. We prayed together and in that moment, I felt calm and peaceful. I knew what I had to do in order to become focused on my goals. I learned that much of my confusion came from the abandonment of my biological father and my need to know who I was. I was angry and confused by this, although I had a man who was a father to me from day one. I began to look at the more positive aspects of my life, knowing that someday I would have more answers than questions. All in due time. I decided that once I returned home, I would commit myself to being more faithful and trusting in what God had in store for me.

Since I've been back home, I have been chasing two dreams

that sometimes can knock heads with each other; writing and dancing. These two passions were both developed at an early age. Most people have only recognized one of my passions, dance, but I blame myself for making it seem as though dancing were all I could do.

I've been dancing probably since I was in my mother's womb. I can't remember exactly how far back, but growing up, I would watch Michael Jackson and try to master every single step in every song, video, and movie he was in. I watched him for years and years and soon, became an artist myself. I started to create my own moves with my own style. Any hip hop music video that came on, I made it my business to know it.

My family began to notice and my parents enrolled me in modern dance classes at the Garth Fagan Dance Company. I knew that some of the best dancers in the world were versatile and I definitely wanted to always stay on top of my game.

When I was sixteen years old, I was introduced to an element of hip-hop I had not known about, B-boying or Breakdance, as defined by the media. I fell in love with the culture as it depicted an artistry of dance I could relate to.

I started to battle, compete, and even joined a number of dance crews such as Morgan State Streetlytez, Anbu Clan, DOPE Squad, Ground Control Crew, and currently, SuperNova Dance Crew. I am currently working hard to make a future for myself in dance. I have been making dance videos and posting them on YouTube. I'm performing with my dance crew and I am even going to audition for *So You Think You Can Dance* Season 11 in 2014.

Dance has helped me to express myself and has helped me

to cope with a few things in my life that have left me feeling hopeless. It helps keep my mind calm and keep my sanity strong and intact. I dance because it is me. It is who I am: a dancer. I also plan to give back to the community by someday opening a studio and offering dance lessons for inner city kids, so that they may express who they are. Paying it back and paying it forward have always been lessons that are important to me.

Another major piece of my life that most people don't know about is my love for writing. Growing up, I remember I hated English class, writing papers, and definitely reading. I struggled with comprehension. The confusing part was that as much as I disliked English class, I was always writing short stories and fan fiction. There were even times during class that I was writing short stories in my notebook instead of taking notes.

I soon developed a passion for writing. I have written many short stories and a couple of novels. I am currently working on an eBook series: Book 1 of 4 of *Evanescence*. I have been giving my supporters downloaded samples of the book and so far there has been nothing but positive feedback and a slew of finish it quickly messages. I have been accepted to SUNY Empire State where I will study English and writing, but I also plan to take classes for film and cinematography, with the intent to become a director. I will practice and hone each craft to its fullest potential. With the support of my parents, the strength of my father and the ambition of my mother, I am confident that I can make my dreams a reality.

My journey as a child of a teenage mother is one that I look back on with deep appreciation for all that my mom sacrificed in order for us to have a better life today. I am no longer bitter about the lack of relationship with my biological father, just blessed and grateful for the father God placed in my life when I needed a dad the most. Through my journey thus far, I realize the power of prayer and its importance. I know the main ingredient to a person's success is faith and I know through faith, opportunities for success are endless.

Author's Corner

Biography: Rafael Johnson, oldest child of Cory and Tanishia Johnson, is 23 years old and resides in Rochester, New York. He is best known in Rochester for his artistry in dance and scriptwriting. At an early age, he was introduced to his first love and passion, dance. He credits his passion for dance to his admiration for the artists Michael Jackson and Usher. Because of his passion for dance, he attended Garth Fagan Dance Company where he learned various genres of dance and enhanced his skills. His other talents and portfolio include: drawing and script writing. Rafael attended McQuaid Jesuit Middle and High School for five years on a full academic scholarship. He is a proud graduate of Bishop Kearney High School. In 2008, he attended Morgan State University in Baltimore, Maryland. Seeking to be closer to his family, Rafael returned to Rochester, and is currently completing his bachelor degree studies at Empire College, where he is a dual major in English and script-writing. Rafael continues to hone his dance abilities and will be auditioning for the 2014 season of *So You Think You Can Dance*. In 2010, Rafael auditioned for *America's Best Dance Crew*, with his group Anbu Clan, a dance group known to many in Rochester and the surrounding communities. The group successfully made it to 2nd rounds. It was during this audition where Rafael's interest in dance peaked; at that time he decided to independently pursue dance as a career. Combining his passion for dance and writing, Rafael has enhanced his portfolio to include 14 short stories modeling various genres including: romantic suspense, drama and mystery. An prolific fiction and non-fiction writer, Rafael is completing a book saga titled, *Evanescence*, for which he is currently seeking a publisher.

Rafael is a member of St. Ambrose, Peace of Christ Community and is thankful to his parents for their unconditional love and support and thankful to God for His granting of talents, gifts and blessings. Rafael is inspired by the quote: *You can dream about it or you can go out and make it happen* - Author unknown

Acknowledgments: I would like to first give thanks to God for all my blessings and Jesus Christ, my savior, for walking through this life with me. I would like to thank my mother for staying strong and teaching me to never back down from any hardship that is in front of you. I would like to thank my father, Cory Johnson, who stepped into my life and protected me and taught me so much about being a man, far greater than anyone else. I love you both very much. To my grandmother, thank you for raising me during the time mom was attending college. Thank you for all of your love and support. To Mike and Jackie Campbell, thank you for stepping into my life as grandparents when I truly needed them. I would like to acknowledge and thank Mrs. LaShunda Leslie-Smith for giving me an opportunity to share my story with everyone. Thank you.

Contact Info:
Rafael Johnson
bboyreflex12@gmail.com
Facebook: https://www.facebook.com/flex.johnson.923
Twitter: @bboyralphy
Phone: 585-266-4248

BONUS

TO MY MOTHER
Branden Calloway

Growing up, I don't really remember all the struggles my mother went through while raising me. I've always remembered food on the table, clothes on my back and shoes on my feet. My mother was, and is, an interesting woman. I look at her life and think, "Wow, she's intelligent, an intellectual, honest, loving, diverse, and so much more." She's accomplished more things in her life than some women ever do.

She had a child at the age of 14, graduated high school, went to college, and got her bachelor and master degrees. She started her own business, took things into her hands, and helped young mothers who struggled much like she did. She is the definition of the street term *Boss*. Watching my mother grow up, I learned a lot of things from her. She did all she could to prepare me for the real world. I'm thankful for that. A lot of kids my age and younger don't have parents to look up to. Even though my father wasn't a major player in my life, I had my mother. She was a mother, father, brother and even a sister. I often look back on the things I've done and when things get confusing, I ask myself a simple question,

"What would mom do?" Believe it or not, it always helps me put things in perspective.

My Mother raised me mostly by herself, until my stepfather stepped in. I knew my *real* father, but I didn't have a good relationship with him. He wasn't around much, and it hurt me. I was torn apart as a little kid knowing that my real father knew where I lived, knew my number, but never visited, and rarely called. When he and my mother split, my mother didn't ask him for much of anything. She didn't need him to take care of me, but *I needed him.* I yearned for him.

I remember I'd call him every week, just to see if he could come get me. Sometimes, he did just that. He'd pick me up; he'd buy me shoes and clothes to wear. Sometimes, he even put money in my pocket. In all honesty, I wasn't looking for that. I wanted him to talk to me and show me things—teach me things. You know, do all the things fathers do with their sons. My stepfather did all of this with me, but I paid no attention to it, at first. I wanted my real father to do it. But he didn't. I would cry and cry and cry some more. My mother would be right there, comforting me. It made me feel good to an extent. At least one of the two people that made me loved me. She talked to me and helped me to understand I couldn't make people do what I wanted them to do and that I couldn't control how others acted towards me, I could only control my response towards them. Learning that helped me to respect my step-father. I grew to love him, especially for stepping in and loving another man's child.

My stepfather never had a father; he lost his dad when he was just a baby. He went through his life with no father to look up to. He gave me everything he would have wanted as a kid. I love him for that.

Eventually, I told my father how I felt about his parenting and about how it hurt me. He said he understood me and admitted that his parenting skills weren't the best. Today, my real father and I are cordial. I love him—I'll never stop loving him. I'm grateful my mother helped me to realize that I couldn't spend my days feeling stressed out because my father wouldn't be a part of my life. She helped me see that at the end of the day, I had a life of my own to live.

I spent so much time trying to make things right with my dad, that I forgot how to live—how to enjoy things. So, I acted out sometimes. It was how I coped with the pain of having an absent father. But when I started the ninth grade, I decided to let all of that pain go; I forgave my father. I began focusing more on me and what I wanted to do. And naturally, my mother was right beside me. She got me into whatever program I wanted to be a part of. Any sport I wanted to play, she made sure I played it. My stepfather was my coach, and biggest cheerleader, at every game.

I know you're thinking, "Wow, this kid has some great parents!" Well, you're right. I do. I love them. They support me in every positive thing I want to do with my life. I've learned a lot watching my mother. She's my idol and my inspiration to do better—to be greater. I thank God for her. I thank her for enduring through all the things she went through just so that I could have a better life than the one she had. I thank God for creating her with such character traits as being dedicated, having a loving spirit, and being a good leader. He made her stronger through her struggles and because of that, she never gave up on me or her family.

Author's Corner

Biography: Son of LaShunda Leslie-Smith, Branden Calloway is a talented musician and artist, and has a vast interest in photography. Branden recently completed his freshmen year of college and is exploring all that life has to offer. This is Branden's first experience as an author and he hopes to continues on the path that God has set before him.

Acknowledgments: I'd like to thank my mother for this opportunity to share my story in her book. I love you for all that you've done in my life, for all the opportunities you've given me and for being a good mother to my sister and me. I thank my step-father for stepping into my life and doing everything my biological father couldn't do at the time. I thank him for helping my mother through her struggles and helping her to become the woman she is today.

Contact Info:
Branden Calloway
Branden_calloway@yahoo.com

Contact Information
for Speaking Engagements and Workshops

Interested in contacting the authors for your next conference, speaking engagement, or television program?

You can do so by emailing us at learnmore@lashundalesliesmith.com.

LaShunda Leslie-Smith, LMSW
PO Box 19412
Rochester, NY 14619
www.journeyofateenagemother.com
www.lashundalesliesmith.com
lls@lashundalesliesmith.com
Facebook: https://www.facebook.com/llesliesmith
Twitter: @llesliesmith
LinkedIn: LaShunda Leslie-Smith, LMSW
585-309-2283 Phone
585-436-6219 fax

ENDNOTES

Chapter 3: [i] Lino, Mark. April 1996. *Expenditures on Children by Families*, 1995 Annual Report. U.S. Department of Agriculture, (Center for Nutrition Policy and Promotion, Washington, D.C.) Publication No. 1528-1995.

Chapter 8: [ii] A more in depth look at this study can be found at: http://news.usc.edu/sexual-Abuse-Teen-Pregnancy/

Chapter 12: [iii] http://www.ourbabynamer.com/meaning-of-Nakisha.html